Santa Claus
Vol. 3
COLLECTION

*"Faith is believing in things when
common sense tells you not to."*
—Miracle on 34th Street
Photograph by Scott Little

"How dreary would be
the world if there were
no Santa Claus!"

—*Francis P. Church 1897*

From the Lenore Santi collection. ✦ *Photograph by Perry Struse.*

Better Homes and Gardens® Creative Collection™
Des Moines, Iowa

The Kindly Spirit

Though Santa Claus may seem reclusive, sequestered in his North Pole retreat for most of the year and moving from home to home under the cover of night on Christmas Eve, his ageless aura permeates the yuletide season. Whether we call this spirit Saint Nicholas, Kris Kringle, St. Nick, Sinterclaus, the jolly old elf, or simply Santa, he embodies the best part of a joyful holiday and inspires our most generous instincts. For the *Santa Claus Collection, Volume 3*, we looked for people, projects, and lore that exemplify the giving spirit that is Santa Claus and brought them all together in the pages of this book.

The kindly spirit of Santa Claus touches people in many ways. His legend, filled with tales of sharing and kindness, has endured—and grown—for nearly eighteen centuries. Even the movies bring us tales of Santa's infectious goodness. The artisans featured here are more than carvers, painters, and sculptors—they share a mission to personify the essence of Santa Claus. Passionate collectors are as interested in the mystique of Santa as they are in the items they've purchased and the beautiful displays they create. Why not participate in the spirit of Santa yourself by crafting a Santa Claus with your hands—and your heart?

Within the pages of the *Santa Claus Collection, Volume 3*, you'll find all the resources you need to capture—and share—Santa's kindly spirit. You'll find the reason to…

Believe!

Table of Contents

Kathy Patterson of Paris,
Ontario, creates reproductions
of old German Santas.

Left: *Chocolate molds from another era shape these*
Walnut Ridge Collectibles Santas.

LASTING LEGENDS

Santa Claus has a long history, drawn from many sources. Each tale of the beloved gift-giver only enhances his mystique.

In the 1830s "A Visit from Saint Nicholas," Clement Moore's classic poem introduced Santa's eight reindeer: Dasher, Dancer, Prancer, Vixen, Comet, Cupid, Donder, and Blitzen. The existence of Rudolph wasn't known until 100 years later.

It's easy to believe you're at the North Pole instead of Anniston, Alabama, when you share cookies and milk with Santa and Mrs. Claus (a.k.a. Bill and Pat Veazey).

Santa & Mrs. Claus

AS SANTA AND MRS. CLAUS, BILL AND PAT VEAZEY ENCHANT CHILDREN AND GROWN-UPS ALIKE WITH THEIR MERRY MELODIES AND WARM SOUTHERN CHARM.

Santa leaves Rudolph at home and hops a helicopter for his annual visit to Carraway Methodist Medical Center in Birmingham, Alabama. Youngsters who attend day care here wiggle with anticipation inside the hospital's huge hangar.

Their faces brighten as the air-ambulance descends and they see Santa and Mrs. Claus waving. "When he gets off that helicopter and starts walking toward the children, their faces are just more than aglow," says Cindy Cook, manager of the day-care center for the children of hospital employees. "They all run up and hug him."

Of course, Santa's timeless magic charms grown-ups as well. Adults crowd the hospital windows for a peek. One doctor hasn't missed a year in the 17 that Santa has appeared here,

Written by Kellye Carter Crocker ✦ Photographs by Craig Anderson

Cindy says. "He says, 'You know, I love Christmas and when this happens every year, I know that Christmas has really arrived.'"

NO ORDINARY ST. NICK

Bill Veazey is the bearded great-grandfather in the familiar red suit spreading cheer at the Carraway hospital and dozens of other locations each December. But Bill is no ordinary St. Nick.

Along with welcoming children to his lap, listening to wish lists, and sorting out who's been naughty and who's been nice, Bill also sings—much to the delight of everyone within earshot.

He met his wife, Pat, when both were college students studying music at Jacksonville State University in Jacksonville (about 75 miles northeast of Birmingham). His baritone melds with her soprano as the couple croons such favorites as "Silver Bells," "Winter Wonderland," and "Have Yourself a Merry Little Christmas." Recorded background music and a small keyboard accompany them. Their state-of-the-art PA system is parked nearby in a Radio Flyer wagon.

Shelley Stewart recalls rushing through a Birmingham mall one December day when she heard singing. "I was tired and I was in a hurry, but I just had to stop in my tracks because it was so uplifting," she says.

Shelley, who was back home in Birmingham for a visit after moving to Iowa, was delighted to discover that Bill and Pat were the mall music-makers. Shelley had attended church where Bill served as the minister of music. "You talk about singing," Shelley marvels. "He and his wife have two of the most beautiful voices I've ever heard."

Left: *There's always a Mr. and Mrs. Claus duet when Bill and Pat visit a group of children. Afterward, you get to sit on Santa's or Mrs. Claus's lap and review your list.*

Opposite: *Just like at the North Pole, there's a sleigh parked on the Veazeys' front porch in Anniston, Alabama.*

"It's hard for me to even remember when I wasn't Santa," says Bill Veazey. His snow-white beard assures a young admirer he's genuine.

Each Sunday in December, Bill dressed in full Santa regalia to lead the congregation in carols. "He was one of the main things I missed when I moved," Shelley says.

BRING SANTA, TOO

Fans can thank Bill's hometown for steering him toward his Santa path. When Bill grew a beard to celebrate Anniston's centennial, folks ribbed him about how much he looked like the jolly old elf.

At that time, Bill worked for the state's Social Security Administration division. Wondering if playing Santa could help improve the relationship between his department and the local medical community, he visited hospitals, nursing homes, and child-care centers dressed as Santa. That was about 20 years ago.

He returned the following year with his own choir of coworkers. By the third year, Santa Bill had entertained more than 100 groups across Alabama.

His appearances helped him get a foot in the door to see doctors and hospital administrators. "I could walk in any time of the year," Bill says, "and they'd say, 'Well, hey, Santa, come on in!'"

Bill later moved to Montgomery to work for the state's health department. "Could you bring Santa, too?" his new boss asked. Bill retired four years ago, but Santa keeps singing. For nine years Bill worked a grueling 60- to 70-hour week as a mall Santa. He enjoyed the children, but even Santa Claus gets tired at that pace.

Nowadays Bill entertains at office and country club parties, museum receptions, hospitals, nursing homes, car dealerships—anywhere someone needs a singing Santa. He also models for advertisements and works with a photographer who makes holiday portraits.

Bill loves doling out his business card, which resembles a driver's license. This "International Sleigh License" lists Santa's weight as "plump & jolly."

A RELUCTANT MISSUS

For a long time, Pat resisted Bill's urging to play Mrs. Claus. The promise of a helicopter ride to the Carraway hospital finally convinced her to give it a try.

After her first appearance, Pat quickly understood her special role. Some of the bigger boys, around 8 or 9, felt too "grown-up" to sit on Santa's lap but enjoyed chatting with her. Toddlers and shy children, especially, preferred to cuddle in her lap next to the "big guy." If a scared child hangs back, Pat acts as intermediary, saying in her soft drawl, "Darlin', you come and tell Mrs. Claus what you want. I'll tell Santa for you."

Cindy, the day-care manager, says the Veazeys clearly enjoy the children as much as the children enjoy them. "When you meet them for the first time you just know they're good as gold," she says, "just a glowing couple who genuinely care about people."

Pat and Bill, whose car license plate reads "SLEIGH," celebrate Christmas year-round. Some 600-plus Santa figures brighten their home, joined by Santa mugs, pitchers, tins, and plates. Nearly every day, Bill wears a touch of candy-cane red. With his naturally white wavy hair and full beard, even when he's not dressed as Santa, people recognize him.

When the couple vacationed in England, a crowd even descended on them at Buckingham Palace to take photos of "Father Christmas."

"It's that way everywhere I go," Bill says good-naturedly. "It's hard for me to even remember when I wasn't Santa."✦

A collection of Santa Claus ornaments adorn Bill and Pat Veazey's Christmas tree.

Santa's Helpers

SANTA HAS A BIG JOB, BUT THROUGH THE AGES, A VARIETY OF ASSISTANTS—FROM BELSNICKLES TO BELL RINGERS— HAVE HELPED HIM GET IT DONE.

In many German-American communities, Belsnickles were holiday
mischief makers, dressed in masks and clownlike apparel. These three were
photographed in Lancaster County, Pennsylvania, about 1914.

When it's time to deliver Christmas presents to children around the world, Santa is the star. Helping him shine, well, that's the job of a loyal cast of assistants.

Santa's earliest companions weren't the friendly folks we think of today. In fact, ancient European figures such as the Belsnickle and Black Peter were so menacing that they make the modern-day Grinch seem almost cuddly.

SCARY SERVANTS

Many of the devilish sidekicks who accompanied Saint Nicholas on his rounds carried switches for disciplining wayward children; others had baskets in which to whisk away naughty tykes. Among them were Belsnickles, who appeared in German-immigrant neighborhoods in 19th-century America and questioned children about their behavior during the past year.

As with all folklore, early stories of these stern assistants traveled to other countries where they were often

Written by Kellye Carter Crocker

Black Peter accompanied Saint Nicholas in a 1952 Dutch parade.
He carried a bundle of switches, an empty bag to put bad children in,
and a bag of gifts for good children.

Photograph courtesy of the Hulton-Deutsch Collection/CORBIS

reshaped and adopted into local custom. Because of this blending, it's nearly impossible to trace the exact origins of many holiday stories, says Ken Erickson, director of the Center for Ethnographic Research at the University of Missouri–Kansas City.

For example, another assistant, Black Peter, sometimes carried his own list of children who had been bad that year—and he handed out spanking rods to their parents. Though he's associated with Dutch tradition, Jeannette Hart grew up with him in the Czech Republic. She remembers Black Peter stalking dark streets with Saint Nicholas on Feast Day. Of course, as a child, she didn't realize that adults merely were playing these roles. She just knew that Black Peter looked frightful—dressed in dirty black clothes, covered with fur, and sporting a devil's tail and horns.

"It was scary," says Jeannette, who lives in suburban Denver, Colorado. "Santa, he's giving the presents and Black Peter, he's going to the bad kids with coal. My mom said if we were bad, he would take us away. He would put us in a bag." She laughs now, but Jeannette took care not to scare her own son with such stories.

Nevertheless, her 10-year-old, Luca Baccega, is well versed in Black Peter's ways. "He steals your presents," Luca warns. "You don't want to mess with him because he can give you curses that won't go away."

The existence of the ninth reindeer was
revealed by Montgomery Ward stores in
this 1939 complimentary booklet.

FOUR-FOOTED FLYERS

Some early paintings portray Saint Nicholas astride a white horse, a companion who may have been inspired by the Vikings. Their white-bearded god, Odin, came to earth every December on his eight-legged flying steed, Sleipnir, who ran faster than the wind.

As Saint Nicholas evolved into Santa Claus, though, he needed faster transportation. Santa's eight tiny reindeer debuted in the 1823 publication of an anonymous poem, "A Visit from Saint Nicholas," in the Troy, New York, *Sentinel*. The now-famous verse was later attributed to Clement Clarke Moore, a divinity professor who penned the story to amuse his own children for Christmas in 1822.

The "most famous reindeer of all," Rudolph, wouldn't light up the North Pole until 100 years later. Robert L. May, a copywriter for the Montgomery Ward department store company, created the lovable misfit for a booklet first distributed to holiday shoppers in 1939. In 1949, Gene Autry's recording of "Rudolph the Red-Nosed Reindeer" sold 2 million copies. An animated television special, narrated by Burl Ives, appeared in 1964.

THE MISSUS

A kindly, supportive Mrs. Claus appears in the Rudolph special and other holiday TV shows. Those programs don't, however, reveal the apparent spunkiness of the Mrs. Claus introduced in a Victorian-era book.

This 1890s vintage illustration is titled Visit from St. Nick. *Although the title is abbreviated, the images of a sleigh and reindeer are clearly inspired by Clement's Moore's poem.*
Illustration courtesy of Bettman/CORBIS

In the mid-20th century, Santa and Mrs. Claus often were portrayed
as the picture of domestic tranquility.

Photograph courtesy of Bettman/CORBIS

Kit Carter-Weilage, an antique-toy collector from
Louisville, Kentucky, discovered a copy of the book
Goody Santa Claus on a Sleigh-Ride about 10 years ago
while traveling in Europe. Teacher and author
Katharine Lee Bates, who wrote "America, the Beautiful,"
also penned Goody Claus's story, published in 1889 by
the D. Lothrop Company in Boston. "It's a delightful
book," says Kit, who sold it to a private collector.

In 30 pages of verse and fanciful drawings, Mrs. Claus
gently admonishes her spouse, "Why should you have
all the glory of the joyous Christmas story, and poor
little Goody Santa Claus have nothing but the work?"

Often she reveals decidedly non-Victorian views about
the role of women. "Bend your cold ear, Sweetheart Santa,
down to catch my whisper faint: Would it be so very
shocking if your Goody filled a stocking, just for once?
Oh dear! Forgive me. Frowns do not become a saint."

LITTLE ASSISTANTS

Stories of elves have a long history, and not all sprites
are as helpful as the North Pole variety. The Danish
Julenisse, for example, lived in homes and farms and
was said to become quite mischievous if the customary
rice pudding wasn't left for him on Christmas Eve.

Although the modern-day Santa evolved from the
real Saint Nicholas, bishop of Myra, in Clement
Moore's poem, Santa himself is dubbed "a right jolly
old elf" and mid-19th-century illustrations frequently
portray a diminutive figure.

Thomas Nast, whose political-cartooning career spanned the last half of the 19th century, brought Moore's vision to life, drawing the portly Santa we know and designating the North Pole as his home. In Nast's famous Christmas cartoons, Santa often appeared with Mother Goose and her nursery-rhyme characters, but he was a solitary worker.

The Wizard of Oz author, L. Frank Baum, gave Santa elfin helpers. In 1902, he published a fanciful children's book, *The Life and Adventures of Santa Claus*, creating a pseudo biography of Neclaus, an infant rescued and raised by a woodland nymph with the aid of fairies and related creatures. Illustrations in the book picture elflike characters who assist him as he evolves as an immortal gift maker and giver.

CONTEMPORARY HELPERS

Of course, Santa's assistants also take human form. What happens when a child notices that the Santa at the mall looks different from the Santa ringing the charity bell outside? Why, parents explain, those guys are probably Santa's helpers. The real Santa is busy getting the toys and sleigh ready.

And what about people who take time to remember those who are less fortunate? They offer a smile to the downhearted, food to the hungry, and toys to children who otherwise would go without. Perhaps these are Santa's best helpers of all. ◆

The mythical creatures who assist Santa Claus in
L. Frank Baum's 1902 book, The Life and Adventures
of Santa Claus, *bear a strong resemblance to elves.*
Illustration courtesy of Random House Value Publishing, Inc.

"A right jolly
old elf"

*Photograph by
Craig Anderson*

TIMELESS MOVIE CLASSICS
BRING SANTA LORE TO LIFE
AND CELEBRATE SANTA'S
GENEROUS SPIRIT.

Silver-Screen Santas

S omewhere between childhood and adulthood,
the mysteries of Santa Claus challenge common
sense: How can reindeer fly? How does Santa
manage to squeeze down the chimney? The silver
screen has taken the answers and turned them into
stunning stories of wit, wisdom, and inspiration.

Each interpretation engages audiences in familiar
scenes of North Pole doings, thrilling themes of
good versus evil, and lessons in generosity, hope, and
humanity. Despite their variations in plot, Santa movies
share a common theme: Santa Claus is larger than life,
and so are the values he represents.

PROOF

Perhaps the most revered movie of all is *The Miracle on
34th St.* (1947), the heartwarming tale of a Macy's
department-store Santa (played by Edmund Gwenn)
whose "delusion" as Kris Kringle lands him in court to
prove himself or be institutionalized. Part of the battle
is convincing his employer, Doris Walker (Maureen
O'Hara), and her daughter, Susan (Natalie Wood),
that every human being has a need for fantasy.

Everything about him seems real. Santa's beard is
authentic. He communicates with an orphaned Dutch
girl who doesn't speak English. And he wins the hearts
of Macy's customers, putting the Christmas spirit ahead

Written by Judith Stern Friedman

of commercial gain. Ultimately, Santa's case is dismissed when post-office personnel deliver mountains of mail addressed to Santa at the courthouse. The story presents a convincing case not only for believing in Santa Claus but also for believing in our dreams and in ourselves.

In the 1947 Santa Claus classic The Miracle on 34th St., *Kris Kringle teaches skeptics Susan Walker (young Natalie Wood) and her mother (Maureen O'Hara) that "Faith is believing in things when common sense tells you not to."*

A LIVING LEGEND

Although *The Miracle on 34th St.* offers "authoritative evidence" of Santa's existence, other interpretations spark imagination. *Santa Claus: The Movie* (1985) explains Santa's beginnings as a gentle old wood-carver in a "certain time and place." When he and his wife are caught in a blizzard while delivering toys to the village children, they're transported by the North Star to a *vandecum* (elf) castle. Here the wood-carver (David Huddleston) discovers his destiny as the ageless Santa and with the help of the elves, he learns the routine.

As centuries pass, Christmas commercialism again rears its ugly head. Santa, discouraged by the waning spirit, says, "People don't seem to care about giving a gift just to see the light of happiness in a friend's eyes."

Even his free-spirited elf assistant, Patch (Dudley Moore), becomes dispirited and is replaced by another more "elf-conscious" helper. Determined to regain his rapport with Santa, Patch leaves the castle to work for conniving toy tycoon BZ (John Lithgow). The plot thickens when Patch's magic candy-cane formula backfires and becomes dangerous to boys and girls everywhere. BZ's stepniece, Cornelia, and her orphan friend, Joe, overhear the plot to sell the treats anyway, and they solicit Santa's help to save the day.

Santa Claus: The Movie skillfully blends reality and fantasy, with impressive special effects, such as magical stardust and food with the power to make reindeer fly. On another level, it shows Santa's human side when he befriends the lonely orphan boy. He recognizes the talents of his *vandecum* associates and eventually works out his differences with Patch.

HUMBLE HERO

The 1966 film *The Christmas That Almost Wasn't* explores Santa's spirit from another perspective. In this light-hearted melodrama, Mr. Phinias T. Prune (played by Rossano Brazzi) is out to foreclose on Santa's workshop. Santa (Alberto Rabagliati) enlists help from lawyer Sam

Whipple (Paul Tripp), who devises a plan to make the payment by going to work for Prim's department store.

Their efforts fail, however, when the evil Mr. Prune buys out Prim, fires Santa and Whipple, and confiscates all the money they've earned. In a last-ditch attempt to save Christmas—just hours before the midnight flight—Santa tells his plight to a passing boy and, miraculously, the village children appear with piggy-bank offerings. "It's time the children do something for you," the boy insists.

This warming tale of give and take also sends a message about forgiveness. Although Santa is victimized by Prune, he remains kind and generous to the end. Santa even delivers a long-lost toy boat to Prune, who finally enjoys the true spirit of Christmas. The movie's closing credit perfectly captures the spirit: "All characters are fictitious except Santa Claus."

In The Christmas That Almost Wasn't, *Santa and Mrs. Claus prepare to to make their holiday trip.*

THE HUMAN EXPERIENCE

Walt Disney Pictures' 1994 movie *The Santa Clause* offers a contemporary twist on Santa, as Scott Calvin (played by Tim Allen) reluctantly becomes the jolly hero—after the real Santa falls off a roof.

In desperation, the single father sharing custody of his son, Charlie (Eric Lloyd), dons Santa's suit to save the evening. "The reindeer will know what to do," says the business card tucked inside the old man's pocket. Father and son are swept away to the North Pole, where they meet the elves, help pack the sleigh, and take off across the sky to deliver the toys. When

In the 1994 film The Santa Clause, *Scott Calvin (Tim Allen) and his son Charlie (Eric Lloyd),* below, *have a Christmas Eve encounter with Santa Claus that causes Scott to mysteriously acquire the jolly old elf's appearance and physique,* above.

Photographs courtesy of the Disney Enteprises, Inc. © Disney Enterprises, Inc.

morning dawns, the whole experience appears to be a dream, except for Scott's red silk pajamas embroidered with "SC."

Enter Scott's ex-wife, Laura (Wendy Crewson), and her psychiatrist boyfriend, Neal (Judge Reinhold), who resent Scott for filling Charlie with fantasies. Yet Charlie insists that Santa is real. Laura and Neal are forced to fight for custody, while Scott and Charlie stand their ground. The audience is asked yet again to question, "What does it take to believe?"

Meanwhile, Scott gains 45 pounds in a week and can't keep the whiskers from growing on his chin. His gradual transformation into Santa and the unwavering support he receives from his son give him reason to believe in himself—and to suggest that Santa exists in everyone.

CELEBRATING SANTA'S STORY

These Santa movies are but a sampling of the many entertaining Christmas films available. Whatever the plot and whether documentary or fantasy, Santa movies unfailingly renew our belief in what is good. The question isn't whether Santa exists or even how he squeezes down the chimney but rather how we celebrate his story. And the movies are the perfect medium, bringing people together, inspiring wonder, and creating a time-honored holiday tradition.✦

*These diminutive Saint Nicholas figures
were once candy containers, filled with
holiday treats for a good little boy or girl.
—Photograph by Perry Struse*

There's more to collecting
Santa Claus than figurines.
For more than a century,
the jolly old elf has appeared
on a myriad of items that are
now treasured collectibles.

TIMELESS
MEMORABILIA

Candy Containers

ON CHRISTMASES PAST,
WHEN THE LITTLE CANDY GIFTS
INSIDE WERE GONE AND
FORGOTTEN, THE CONTAINERS
THEY CAME IN TOOK ON
A NEW LIFE AND VALUE
ALL THEIR OWN.

Early German candy containers depicted Santa on a donkey or sleigh, an elf sitting on a log, a child with a bisque head pushing a papier-mâché snow-box sled, a cornucopia with a gold foil cone, and even a Santa sitting on a composition bombshell during wartime.

Because of their papier-mâché and composition makeup, the containers fit into the ephemera category, those paper-based materials now worth far more than the paper they were printed on or made from. Ephemera encompasses a wide range of artifacts, most originally intended for one-time or short-term use.

Santa Claus was a favorite design among late 19th- and early 20th-century German candy-container makers.

Written by Carol McGarvey ◆ Photographs by Perry Struse

*German candy containers were made
in a variety of sizes. The bucket style
at center front is very rare.*

Above: *Even simple box candy containers show elaborate detail.*

Opposite: *Designed to be discarded or used as short-term toys, German-made candy containers have survived for 80 years or more.*

Although many antiques guides report that candy containers were officially introduced to mass audiences as Liberty Bell-shape containers during the Centennial Exposition of 1876, collector Kit Carter-Weilage of Louisville, Kentucky, insists that some containers were made in Germany in the 1860s. Germans produced the containers in great numbers until about 1920.

A NEW ERA

"After World War I, craftsmanship in Germany eroded immeasurably," Kit explains. Part of it had to do with specific papier-mâché formulas being lost. And for economy, the Germans began adding sawdust and straw to their mixtures, so the consistency changed.

Most of the candy containers were exported from Germany and purchased by wealthy Americans, she says. "After children ate the candies inside, they often attached the containers to the Christmas trees as decorations and ornaments. Likely, the containers cost from $1.50 to $20, certainly a lot of money in those times, so they were given only in wealthy circles."

After Christmas, the containers became toys. "Considering that they were playthings for children and weren't made of sturdy materials to begin with, it's just amazing that so many have survived," says the Louisville collector, who describes herself as a "weekend warrior" when it comes to antiques.

One collector who's been smitten by the containers for the past 18 years is Scott Tagliapietra, an antiques dealer from southern Wisconsin. "When I was a child, I went with my mother to auctions all over northern Wisconsin. I bought boxes of old Christmas items that nobody else wanted. *Now* they do," he says.

Scott loves all kinds of Christmas items, from antique ornaments to Santa games to feather trees. He figures he has about 75 German candy containers. "Likely,

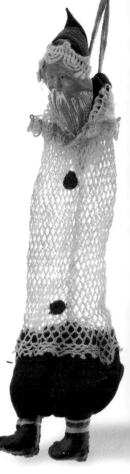

German families didn't have these in their homes. Most were sent to the United States," he explains.

Margot Burnham of Des Moines, Iowa, who was born in Germany and who designs and fashions German Christmas angels, confirms that. "I've heard of the containers, but I've never seen them. Indeed, most likely nearly all of them were exported."

Scott shows off many of his holiday treasures year-round, displaying them in cases in his den. Christmas is his favorite holiday for pull-out-all-the-stops decorating, but he also collects Halloween and Easter trims and ornaments.

Of candy containers, he says he never comes across the same ones twice.

DATING CONTAINERS

Kit points out that in Germany, making candy containers was always a cottage industry. "One person would make the papier-mâché, one would work with the molds, one would detail the body and accessories, and the masters would paint the faces. The details around the eyes and the realistic skin tones would show off their skill and attention to their craft. Some painters even became ambidextrous to get more done in a day."

She also notes that it's common to date the containers earlier or later than they actually might have been made. "A dour demeanor on Santa's face would indicate an earlier container. It wasn't until after Thomas Nast started painting happy, rotund Santa faces that the Germans followed suit. That's one way of dating the containers."

Candy containers were made in various sizes, from 5 to about 40 inches tall. It's important to take note of the closure when examining them. Containers with screw tops may actually be perfume holders and other miniatures.

Kit's looking for the one container she's never found. "I sell about 95 percent of what I purchase, mostly at seven shows a year around the country." Although she doesn't deal in any items made after about 1920, she knows there are collectors who focus on another genre of candy containers—those from the 1950s.

Right: Mesh bags, with figural heads and feet, were inexpensive when new.

Opposite: After World War II, candy-container production shifted to Japan, where containers were made in factories.

THE '50s

Remember those Christmas stocking shapes filled with candies and small plastic toys from the five-and-dime? They were made of see-through red mesh, much like the bags onions come in. Along with a growing number of plastic Christmas items and various candy containers from the post-World War II era, they were made in Japan. Much less expensive in nature, they're favorites among collectors of 1950s memorabilia. Some of the plastic collectibles include Santa on skis, felt-covered cardboard Santa boots, and Disney characters.

Contemporary ornament designer Christopher Radko has worked since 1988 at re-creating vintage German Santas and holiday candy containers that feature old patterns. Each edition is limited to 600 pieces signed by the artist.

Scott says he appreciates Radko's attention to detail. "However, they're still not the same as the originals, even though, at some time in the future, I suppose they'll be collectible as well."

"Being caretakers of items from the past is very special," Scott emphasizes. "It's just the whole aura of Christmas Past that's so charming. It's becoming a lost art, and we must protect it."

Kit couldn't agree more. "When you acquire a Christmas piece from long ago, you're not just buying an item, you're becoming the custodian of the soul of all those who've loved it before you."✦

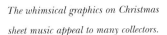

The whimsical graphics on Christmas sheet music appeal to many collectors.

Santa in Song

THESE LONGTIME FRIENDS ARE SPREADING HARMONY THROUGH THEIR SANTA-MUSIC COLLECTIONS.

Once a year, jingle bells ring and familiar Christmas tunes help us celebrate the spirit of the season. For some, however, the music plays year-round. These are the folks who've chosen to honor Santa and the holiday by collecting vintage Christmas sheet music and record albums.

Bob and Sandy Fellows treasure their collection in their Branchburg, New Jersey, home. In just six years, they've aquired Christmas albums, children's records, sheet music, and player-piano rolls. During the holidays, their two jukeboxes play only Christmas music.

Written by Judith Stern Friedman ✦ *Photographs by Perry Struse*

Gene Autry, affectionately known as "The Singing Cowboy," could also be dubbed the "King of Christmas Music."

their passion. "We realized all the neat things we have," Sandy says.

On one piece of music, a whimsical Santa with his bagful of toys confirms the giving spirit. On another, a detailed pen-and-ink drawing depicts a happy family around the tree. Some record albums showcase performers who've become Christmas legends. Gene Autry's 1947 release of "Here Comes Santa Claus," the British group Stargazers singing "I Believe in Santa Claus" (1950), and Jimmy Boyd's 1952 performance of "I Saw Mommy Kissing Santa Claus" all became part of Santa's lore.

RUDOLPH'S ROUTE

Both collectors will tell you that the history of Santa music is inextricably linked to children. The timeless

Nearby, in Westfield, New Jersey, Tony Annese owns thousands of Christmas record jackets and albums, some of which hang seasonally on the walls of his home. "I'm attracted to the presentation," Tony says. "I like visual things."

These avid collectors who've known each other for several years, eventually discovered a way to share the joy their hobby brings. They put their collections on display at the annual Golden Glow of Christmas Past convention, where collectors of vintage Christmas memorabilia from across the nation convene every summer to fuel

Though Gene Autry was the first to record "Rudolph the Red-Nosed Reindeer," he was far from the last.

classic about Santa's helper, "Rudolph the Red-Nosed Reindeer," was written in verse in 1939 specifically for children by Montgomery Ward copywriter Robert L. May. Department-store Santas gave away more than 2.4 million comic-book versions of the story—and another 3.6 million reissues in 1946. When the copyright was reassigned to May in 1947, Rudolph's popularity continued through his appearance on watches, clothing, ornaments, mugs, and other promotional items.

Not until 1949 were the Rudolph lyrics set to music by May's brother-in-law, Johnny Marks. Gene Autry's 78-rpm recording of the song, released September 19, 1949, became the number-two best-selling Christmas hit of all time ("White Christmas" is number one).

Furthering Rudolph's popularity in the early 1950s, the Bradford Plastic Company created "record riders," which were sold with the 78s. A three-dimensional Rudolph figure was glued to a 3-inch-diameter disk that rotated when placed on a record-player spindle.

In the 1950s, children's records took on new forms. Some, like "Santa's 10 Rules," above center, *came with brightly decorated mailing envelopes.*

According to Sandy and Bob, other nontraditional music memorabilia followed. Free-form-shape records doubled as gift cards or postcards and played "Santa Claus Is Coming to Town." Other picture disks made of cardboard and vinyl were imprinted with colorful holiday motifs, and still others were cut into Santa Claus shapes.

GRAPHIC APPEAL

For the first 50 years after Thomas Edison's 1877 invention (originally on tinfoil records), recordings were made for a specific brand of player. After standardized 78-rpm records were introduced in the 1930s, striking jacket designs followed (and later for 45s). "These records were smaller than the 33⅓-rpm LPs that came later," Sandy says. "They really had to catch the eye."

The sheet music of the 1950s took a similar graphic approach. "Some of the music had Santa on the cover, even if he had nothing to do with the song," Bob observes. "People would buy it just because they related it to Christmas."

Besides advertising the tunes, music graphics also reflected the times. Sheet music was made smaller during World War I so families could save when they shipped it to soldiers overseas. On the sheet music for Eddie Howard's 1947 "Dearest Santa," a simple statement reads: "Dedicated to Placement Bureau of the New York Foundling," an appropriate sentiment for a needy orphanage.

According to Tony, colorful picture sleeves blossomed in the 1950s, when emphasis shifted to the records' visual presentation. As post-WWII babies were growing up, "Companies were trying to sell music to children, for parents to buy," Tony explains.

THE THRILL OF THE HUNT

Starting at 50 cents and averaging just a few dollars each, most vintage Christmas albums and sheet music are very affordable. The better the condition, the higher the price. You should never buy something just because you think it will increase in value, Sandy warns: "Buy it because you like it."

Die-hard collectors comb garage sales, flea markets, and ephemera, record, and antiques shows for pieces to add to their growing collections. Holiday music is available year-round, although it's sometimes difficult to find in good condition. Seasoned collectors protect their albums and sheet music with plastic sleeves and store them in waterproof boxes, away from humidity—but more importantly, they keep them in a place where they can enjoy them.

For all its engaging formats, expressive graphics, and contributions to Americana—Santa in song is a true inspiration. "With its emphasis on childhood, holiday music evokes a very comfortable feeling," Tony says. "Music is a wonderful way to share your love of Santa and Christmas."✦

Children's holiday records from the '50s show Santa Claus making his appointed rounds on Christmas Eve.

Musical Sentiments for Santa

1930s

"Santa Claus is Coming to Town" (1934)
Gene Autry
"I'm Sending a Letter to Santa Claus" (1939)
Vera Lynn

1940s

"Dearest Santa" (1947)
Eddie Howard
"Here Comes Santa Claus" (1947)
Gene Autry
"I Wish That I Were Santa Claus" (1949)
Bob Kennedy
"Santa, Santa, Santa" (1949)
Gene Autry

1950s

"I Believe in Santa Claus" (1950)
Stargazers
"I Saw Mommy Kissing Santa Claus" (1952)
Jimmy Boyd
"Howdy Doody and Santa Claus" (2-record set) (1953)
Buffalo Bob Smith and Edward Kean

"Santa Got Stuck in the Chimney" (1953)
Jimmy Boyd
"Santa Baby" (1953)
Eartha Kit
"A Christmas Present to Santa Claus" (1954)
Rosemary Clooney
"Santa and the Doodle Li Boop" (1954)
Art Carney
"I'm Gonna Lasso Santa Claus (1956)
Little Brenda Lee
"Santa and the Purple People Eater" (1958)
Sheb Wooley
"Santa's Comin' in a Whirlybird" (1959)
Gene Autry

1960s and Later

"Be a Santa" (1961)
Mitch Miller
"Santa Claus is Watching You" (1962)
Ray Stevens
"Barefoot Santa Claus" (1966)
Sonny James
"To Heck with Ole Santa Claus" (1966)
Loretta Lynn
"Santa's Gonna Come in a Stagecoach" (1971)
Buck Owens and Susan Raye
"Santa Claus is Coming To Town" (1981)
Bruce Springsteen

A vision of Christmas Past
lives on in the hearts and homes
of those who seek—
and treasure—the Santa Claus
ornaments, toys, and images
of days gone by.

DEVOTED COLLECTORS

A beautifully painted Father Christmas clip-on
ornament, circa 1910, wears a peaked cap instead
of a hood. (From the collection of Scott Tagliapetra)
—Photograph by Perry Struse

A Lifetime
of Collecting
Christmas

THIS WISCONSIN
ANTIQUES DEALER
BEGAN COLLECTING
CHRISTMAS AT
AN EARLY AGE—
AND NEVER STOPPED.

O
h, to be Scott Tagliapietra as a boy going
to auctions and flea markets in northern
Wisconsin with his mother! As she searched
for old coffee grinders, spice boxes, and lamps, young
Scott was buying box after box of old Christmas
ornaments. An entire box would set him back only a
few dollars because no one else wanted them. He'd
borrow the money from his mother and organize his
treasures in a glass case that he kept in his bedroom.

Above: *This 10-inch-long turn-of-the-century German papier-mâché Santa
Claus actually is a lantern. A candle can be placed in the back, lighting up
the eyes and mouth.*

Opposite: *The base of Scott's main Christmas tree is as lively as its branches,
with lovingly collected toys, such as a drum depicting a Santa in an airplane,
a Santa jack-in-the-box, and a weighted roly-poly Santa doll.*

Written by Allison Engel ✦ Photographs by Perry Struse

*Rare figural glass ornaments hang on
a feather tree in the entry of Scott's home.
The tree rests on an antique musical
Christmas-tree stand.*

As a teenager, he added to his collection by running classified ads in his local weekly at Christmastime, looking for old ornaments. Clintonville, Wisconsin, was—and is—an area settled by Germans, and he was able to purchase many vintage turn-of-the-century German ornaments for a few dollars each. "People then were happy to get $5 apiece for them," he recalls.

NO REGRETS

Today the figural glass Christmas ornaments he acquired for a song as a child are worth hundreds of dollars each. Scott no longer owns these original finds, but he doesn't regret selling them. He sold them to serious collectors as a way to start his antique-ornament business, Scott's Antiques. Selling those ornaments allowed him to meet the collectors who would become his clients, learn what ornaments they collected, and how much they were willing to spend. Although he also collects vintage toys and items from Easter and Halloween, Scott never has strayed from his first love, Christmas. And he's amassed a personal collection that dwarfs the early purchases he kept in his bedroom.

A TALL TREE

Scott now lives in southern Wisconsin, on a cliff overlooking Lake Michigan. His 1949 home, designed by a protégé of Frank Lloyd Wright, features 18-foot

Santa collector Scott Tagliapietra shows off some of his rare German-made Father Christmas figures.

ceilings, which allow him to set up a 14-foot tree during the holidays. The imposing tree holds hundreds of antique clip-on bird ornaments, clip-on Santas and clowns, and early blown-glass balls with dimples known in the trade as "indents." Around the base of the tree, Scott sets up a tableaux of vintage toys, games, Santas, and stuffed animals.

In the foyer is a small European feather tree that holds his rarest ornaments, including annealed legged ornaments, which are German glass ornaments with stems that have been pulled down to approximate legs. Made at the turn of the 19th century, they were created to resemble popular characters of the day—Mary Pickford, the Keystone Kops, clowns, Indians—and of

This carved walnut Father Christmas nutcracker, found at a Paris flea market, is one of Scott's newer acquisitions. It opens at the mouth, and pressure on the beard and pointed hat cracks the shell.

Left: An ornate German candy container features Santa Claus in a sleigh pulled by a single realistic reindeer.

Opposite: Scott's den has an entire wall of display cases filled with vintage Santa Claus board games, Belsnickle figures, and Santa containers that pull apart to hold candy.

course, Santa Claus. Due to the fragility of the legs, these ornaments are hard to find and expensive, selling for as much as $1,000 each.

A FESTIVE SEASON

Mantels and tabletops throughout Scott's house hold other groupings of antique Christmas items, which he varies every year. This past Christmas, his 10-foot dining-room table held a stunning arrangement of antique Father Christmas figures, holly, and greenery.

Although Scott's business takes him on the road perhaps 35 weeks a year, he arranges to be home at least half of the month of December so he can celebrate the season properly. His trees and ornaments go up Thanksgiving weekend and stay up until the second week of January. He makes it a point to get together with friends at the holiday and always hosts a huge Christmas party.

For his own collection, he seeks out early Father Christmas figures, pre-1910 ornaments, and "anything unusual." He worries that older collectors, who appreciate the skill and personality of turn-of-the-century

handmade ornaments, are being replaced by younger people who prefer mass-produced ornaments from the 1950s and '60s. "The '50s and '60s things were molded and cranked out, but the early German ornaments were a cottage industry, with families working on things together by hand. They were very individualized pieces," explains Scott.

SEARCHING FOR CHRISTMAS

It's nearly impossible to find fine old ornaments coming out of attics at flea markets and auctions these days, Scott says. To find old ornaments of quality, you must buy from other collectors. He travels the country, attending big antiques shows in Atlantic City, New Jersey, and Brimfield, Massachusetts, and goes regularly to Paris on buying trips. "I've always paid a lot for things, but I've always been lucky to find enough people willing to pay even more," he says. Christmas collectors and toy collectors do become more addicted to their hobby than other antiques collectors, Scott believes. "They truly love great items and absolutely have to have them." Still, he notes, "It's a very competitive business, and you wonder every year whether you can keep finding wonderful things."

Why have Christmas items continued to fascinate him for more than three decades? "Everybody seems to me to be happier at Christmas," he says. He readily admits that his Christmases growing up weren't as elaborate as those he celebrates as an adult. "I've sort of dreamed up what Christmas should be, and now I make it special."✦

Forever Santa

THIS AVID SANTA COLLECTOR PROVES YOU'RE NEVER TOO OLD TO BELIEVE.

E very year at holiday time, Lenore Santi's home glows red and white. Hanging from feather trees, posed on shelves, and perched in festive table displays, Santas of every face and form become the dominant decor. "They're just jolly Santas that bring gifts and toys to kids," she explains from her home in a northwest suburb of Chicago.

Her collection encompasses more than 100 jolly men, most dating back at least 50 years, and many over a century. One of her favorite German Santas is stuffed with straw, stiff and stern, but he's nonetheless endearing. "I look for the old ones," Lenore says. "I like their faces." Japanese painted Santa heads, German wire and papier-mâché variations, and even a grouping of English porcelain figures round out the international collection.

Lenore says condition is most important when evaluating collectible Santas. Depending on age, you can overlook some wear and tear.

Written by Judith Stern Friedman ✦ *Photographs by Perry Struse*

Lenore Santi's surname is Italian for saint, which perhaps brings her closer to the lore of St. Nick. "When I look at all these things, they make me smile," she says.

Opposite: *Santas of every shape and size convene in this antique cupboard in Lenore's living room. Her grandchildren love to play with them all, especially the one on roller skates.*

and papier-mâché Santas usually are about 50 or 60 years old, and plastic likenesses are newer.

Although she has her favorites, Lenore handles all her treasures with an affectionate touch. "I've always loved Santa, even as a kid," she says. At 72 years of age, she finds displaying her collection has become a tradition the whole family appreciates. Lenore's husband, David, her 93-year-old mother, two children, three grandchildren, and her sister's family all share the wonder.

Other more recent dolls in Lenore's collection typify the American Santa. With plump, round bellies and billowy beards, one 1950s grouping, probably from Japan, dons pastel pink-, yellow-, and mint-color suits. Some are candles, others are netted candy containers, and newer interpretations light up and sing.

UNCONDITIONAL LOVE

As an avid Santa fan, Lenore isn't particular about the Santas she collects. However, as the number grows, she is becoming more discerning. "When I go out and buy a Santa, it has to be old," she says, "anything over 50 years." She's partial to late-1800s German Belsnickles made of cotton batting and straw, but they're increasingly difficult to find. Vintage cardboard candy containers

This desirable straw-filled Santa is among Lenore's favorites for his stern face, stiff body, and satin suit.

"Jessi (14 years old) and Jake (10 years old) have always counted them for me," Lenore says proudly, "and David (5 years old) really believes in this guy. He leaves out the cookies and the milk." Jolly faces in all directions send a warm message of approval.

ENDURING PURSUIT

Lenore has been collecting Santas for 50 years. She remembers that her first Santa was a blown-glass ornament from Wieboldt's department store. It graced the couple's first Christmas tree after she married David in 1951. Since then, friends and relatives have contributed lots more figures.

A nurse for 30 years, now retired and an antiques dealer for 25, Lenore says, "The majority of these finds were from estate sales, from rummaging through places. I just hit upon them." One mechanical Santa comes from a Chicago convent, and another life-size Santa advertises 7-Up. Lenore found him at a Milwaukee "rummage-o-rama."

Upper left: *This unusual German Santa has a fuzzy wire body and a two-dimensional paper face.* Lower left: *A 100-year-old German Belsnickle with black clogs and brown skirt hangs from a vintage feather tree.*

Clad in a coat of fragile cotton batting, this little German Santa schusses in on a pair of skis.

In 1981, when Lenore and her husband relocated to Whitefish Bay, Wisconsin, she found many treasured German pieces. "Wisconsin is well populated with German families," she explains. Since returning to the Chicago area in 1991, Lenore has continued her estate sale business with her partner, Laverne Masini. She still feels a rush whenever she meets another Santa.

Just after the New Year, Lenore packs up her dolls to replace them with cow creamers and vintage china. Wrapping her Santas delicately in tissue, and placing them on basement storage shelves, she's a bit sad to say good-bye. She knows, however, that the feeling is temporary because next Thanksgiving she'll unveil her dolls again. "We believe in Santa forever," she says. "You know how much you want to."✦

White suits with red trim distinguish these hard-to-find egg-carton Santas from the 1940s and 1950s.

*Rows of molded and painted chalkware Santa
ornaments await finishing touches at Kathi Bejma's
Walnut Ridge Collectibles workshop.
—Photograph by Perry Struse*

MASTER CRAFTERS

For many artisans,
Santa Claus is more than
a Christmas figure.
He's a year-round passion,
a spirit to embody with
wood, clay, paint, fabric,
paper, and a host of
other materials.

Adrift with
Marge Mable

MEET AN IOWA PAINTER WHO COMBINES
THREE PASSIONS INTO A SANTA CLAUS BUSINESS.

Marjorie Wedge Mable perches on a stool
behind the counter at her Folk Art Shop in
West Des Moines, Iowa. She holds a piece of
driftwood in one hand and a paintbrush in the other.
With the easy air of experience, she dips her brush in
a tin of paint, and makes a few strokes on the piece of
driftwood. Before long, a nose appears and then a beard.
In the blink of an eye, a Santa emerges. Meanwhile,
Marge chats with customers, never missing a stroke.

"They're little
ambassadors of love
you're sending out all
over the world."

Written by Debra Landwehr ✦ Photographs by Scott Little and Steve Struse

Marge often paints as she visits with customers in her Folk Art Shop,
where rustic cabinets display rows of Santas. Many carry baskets,
also handwoven by Marge.

"I love to paint and I love people," says Marge, citing
two of the three reasons why she's made almost 5,000
driftwood Santas over the past 16 years. "At first," she
says, "I felt making Santa figures was a bit trite. But
then a friend made a statement I'll never forget."

"They're not just Santas," the friend said. "They're
little ambassadors of love you're sending out all over
the world."

A NATURAL INSPIRATION

Marge made her first driftwood Santa in 1985. As often
happens, this creative inspiration came almost by
accident. Divorced and the mother of five, she and her
daughter Jackie had just opened their shop in West
Des Moines' historic Valley Junction district, filling the
space with their own creations, plus pottery and other
crafts from artisans at nearby Living History Farms.
Marge had been cutting two-dimensional Santas from

From a few inches to a few feet, Marge's driftwood Santas come in every size.

and personality. Before long, she'd made 13 driftwood figures, only using a saw to cut the flat bases.

Tentative, she took them to a juried art show in Pennsylvania; they all sold before noon. Suddenly, Marge had a new endeavor. The American Museum of Folk Art in New York called, requesting a supply of the Santas to sell in their gift shop. An editor from *Better Homes and Gardens® Christmas Ideas* magazine bought several of them to feature in the publication, resulting in orders from all over the world. Suddenly, Marge was in the driftwood-Santa business, sending out her little ambassadors in all directions. But it didn't just change her customers' lives—it changed her life as well.

"I hadn't spent much time on the water since we moved here," Marge says. Now, every Sunday afternoon, she heads to Saylorville Lake north of Des Moines. At first she walked down the back of the dam to collect driftwood in a garbage bag. "I wondered what would happen if I fell in headfirst," she jokes. By the next year, she'd solved that problem: Sales of her Santas enabled her to purchase a boat.

TO BE ON THE WATER

That, in short, is the third reason Marge continues making Santas: to spend more time on the water she loves so much. Every sunny summer day when she's not in the shop, she's out in the boat or paddling around in her kayak, plucking pieces of driftwood from the water and tossing them into a laundry basket or bag in back. "I love pieces that have one end shaped like a Santa hat—formed by beavers chewing on them— or pieces that are perfectly smooth from the sand."

At home, she separates her driftwood finds into separate garbage cans: one for Santas and others for fish, ducks, Lady Liberty, and other figures she makes throughout the year. Another entire can is devoted to twigs she clips from the elm, linden, black walnut, and burr oak trees that populate her backyard. Attached to the Santas with tiny brads, these twigs become

wood and painting them for sale. But one day, a piece of driftwood sitting on a bench at home caught her eye.

"I've always loved the water," Marge says. "I was born in Watertown, New York. We had a camp on the St. Lawrence River, and we lived on a lake in Massachusetts. When she saw the piece of driftwood she'd brought from out East, she realized that it could become a Santa, too. In fact, the wood's rough texture and rugged protrusions would give the character depth

Even though driftwood Santas like this one are Marge's hallmark, she often sees Santa faces hidden in everyday items, below.

blue, and dark green. Recently, her enthusiasm for recycling and her ability to see potential in the most ordinary objects have resulted in new items: She's captured wayward buoys and painted them, too. "They got me interested in painting spheres," she says. "I've painted Santas on golf balls, baseballs, and a kid's bowling ball."

Back at the shop, Marge is finishing the sash on a Santa's suit while she chats with another loyal customer. A 70th birthday, a recent bout with cancer, and a workshop on painting spiritual icons have all deepened her appreciation for the Santas and the original Saint Nicholas, the benevolent bishop on whom the character is based. "It's my ministry," Marge says of her art. "I love painting, people, and water. To work with what I love is incredible." ✦

disproportionately skinny arms, giving the Santas motion and stick-figure charm.

Once the arms are in place, Marge paints the Santas, following a European style that's her own adaptation of several old-world figures. "Every Santa is a different little guy," she says. "For example, the curve at the top of the cheeks can make a smile bigger or smaller."

The final step is to outfit each Santa with a combination of items, including tin stars, baskets, leather bags, and bells. Again, Marge often works afloat on the water, cutting out the stars or weaving the baskets while she sits in the sun on her pontoon. "I use size 0 reed," she says of the baskets, moving her hands through the air and tracing the ins and outs of the weaving. "I've made so many, it's almost automatic."

NEW INSPIRATIONS

Thousands of Santas later, Marge is still intrigued with the figures, although she's made many minor changes along the way. Each year, she chooses a different color for their suits; the most popular colors have been red,

SYLVESTER DIETRICH'S
BASSWOOD CREATIONS
PAINSTAKINGLY REFLECT THE
CHANGING FACE OF SANTA,
FROM STRICT, SOBER SAINT
TO JOLLY OLD ELF.

The
Careful Carver

No matter whether Sylvester Dietrich carves an old-fashioned, somber Saint Nicholas or his jolly modern-day counterpart, he saves the most important work for last: the face. Creases at the eyes, rounder cheeks, and heavier brows all contribute to an array of detailed yet subtle expressions that Sylvester says still challenge him after 20 years of wood carving.

"The key to anything that portends to life is the eyes," he says. "That twinkle in the eyes, I don't get it every time. Carving is a subtractive art, and you don't have much room for error."

TAKING A BREAK

When Sylvester was a kid, everyone urged him to play sports. At 18, the 6-foot 4-inch, 200-pound powerhouse surely would have cast an imposing shadow on the gridiron or the hardwood.

Written by Kellye Carter Crocker ✦ *Photographs by Craig Anderson*

After the coat, hat, and trims
are complete, Sylvester carves
the face of each Santa.

From stern to benevolent—sometimes even whimsical—Sylvester Dietrich's Santas have many different expressions.

Sylvester wasn't interested. He liked crafts. Yet, he didn't try wood carving until the late 1970s while working as a forklift driver for Chrysler in Fenton, Missouri, just west of St. Louis.

During break time at the factory, some workers would exercise, sleep, play cards, or read. A janitor picked up small pieces of wood from around the plant and carved them into guns and other shapes. Intrigued, Sylvester started carving, too. He was 39.

"The first piece I carved was a little Missouri mule," he says. Always fascinated by facial expressions, Sylvester taught himself to carve cowboys, Indians, and hillbillies, as well as birds and animals.

"Never give away your old work. That way, you can tell you've advanced," the artist advises. "You'll look back at an older piece and think, 'I used to think that was good,'" he adds with a laugh.

THE HOBBY THAT GREW

Sylvester carved his first Santa around 1987. While researching the subject, he was amazed to discover that Santa wasn't always the "jolly old elf." Old-time Santas appeared somber, almost stern. "They were as much a figure of discipline as they were of reward," he says.

Each Santa comes with a card explaining its historical significance. "I try to make them representative of the evolution of Santa," he says.

He retired from Chrysler in 1991 and moved to a rural area near New Haven, Missouri (about 65 miles west of St. Louis). Sylvester cleared 15 wooded acres by hand and then built his own home on the land.

He'd planned to carve in retirement, but demand for his work keeps him busier than he ever expected. Collectors ask for new designs every year. "It's a compliment," Sylvester says, "but at the same time, it's an obligation."

His basswood Santas stand 8 to 10 inches tall (one skinny Santa towers to 12 inches), and they sell for about $50 to $60 each.

"It's not a very lucrative business. It's too time-intensive," says Sylvester, who can spend five hours or more just carving a piece. "Basically, I do everything but grow the trees. Originally, I even used to cut down the trees. I use all local wood."

He chuckles when he recalls how, a few years back, a storm sent a large limb crashing onto a local accountant's home. Sylvester traded a pick-up truck full of firewood for the limb and later sold the CPA a Santa carved from his own tree.

A WORKING RETIREMENT

In the morning quiet, Sylvester carves and paints at his dining-room table. He claims 90 percent of the wood chips land in his work apron. (Fortunately, the floor is ceramic tile for easy sweeping, and Shirley, his wife of 40 years, good-naturedly serves the family meals at the big kitchen table.)

Does Santa Claus have a hobby like gardening or fishing?
Some of Sylvester's Santas do!

To make a Santa, Sylvester first cuts a rough figure with a band saw and carefully finishes each piece by hand. The grandfather of 12 admits he's slowing down a bit because the intricate work stresses his hands and arms.

Still, he was able to craft more than 100 pieces last year. His Santa collection includes some 50 styles and variations. Although he uses patterns and ideas modified from other carvers, he also continues to research and experiment with his own designs.

"Each piece an artist makes is usually an extension of himself," Sylvester says. "Every year since '93, I've tried to create a special Santa that I can say is mine."

Carol Eckelkamp, an avid Christmas collector who lives about 30 minutes away in Union, has acquired each of Sylvester's special-edition pieces. Her favorite is the stern yet warm traditional Saint Nicholas dressed in a white robe.

"When I saw his work, I thought he'd captured that nostalgia of the old-world Christmas," says Carol, who displays the figures year-round. "It just reminds me of the Christmases we had as children."

Although he says he's somewhat reclusive, Sylvester travels to two crafts shows each year to sell his carvings. One is in Hermann, an old German river town about 20 miles west. The other, one of the biggest carving shows in the country, is in Belleville, Illinois, across the river from St. Louis. His carvings are also available in two local gift shops.

He also demonstrates his techniques for audiences at crafts shows. "Sometimes I'll take a piece of wood just to see what's in it. When they ask me what it's going to be when I'm finished, the answer is always 'smaller.'" he says with a laugh. ✦

Each Christmas for several years, Sylvester has created a special-edition Santa.

Wood-carvers Joe, left, and Gene Parsons in their Madisonville, Kentucky, home. All her life, Gene has lived within 20 miles of where she was born.

Santas by Two

IF JOE PARSONS HAD
CARVED THE OLD-WORLD
SANTA THAT HIS WIFE, GENE,
WANTED, SHE MIGHT NEVER
HAVE BECOME A CARVER.

Here is a story of love in action. Joe Parsons is a wood-carver from Madisonville, Kentucky, who admits, somewhat reluctantly, that he doesn't understand all the fuss made over his Santa Claus figures. He's carved all his life and vastly prefers to produce Western figures: cowboys, Indians, horses, and that sort of thing. But he's been married for 52 years to a woman named Gene (more on her name later), who dearly loves Santa figures.

So every Christmas, he takes a block of basswood and creates an original Santa just for her. The Santas

A trio of Gene's carved Santas includes a skinny Santa inspired by a thin piece of wood and a potbellied Santa adapted from a rough out block that she purchased at a carving show.

Written by Allison Engel ✦ Photographs by Craig Anderson

MORNING AFTER

Opposite: Gene Parsons' Santas, with angora goat hair beards and one-of-a-kind outfits, are dressed to the nines.

Right: Joe Parsons' intricately carved Santa figures include one holding a wish list, one holding a music box, and one with an elaborate belt buckle.

are usually 10 to 12 inches high and full of clever details. Their faces may be stern or smiling, the hems of their robes may flare out as if caught by the wind, and they may have tiny carved accessories such as backpacks or walking sticks. Joe doesn't make a big deal out of the presentation. When he finishes painting each one, "I just tell her it's hers," he says simply.

"I'LL DO IT MYSELF"

Gene treasures these Santas, and displays them proudly on her mantel. But one year, she saw an old-world Santa in a magazine and she asked Joe to carve it for her. However, Joe wasn't too thrilled with the assignment. In fact, a couple of years went by and Joe still hadn't gotten around to carving that Santa for Gene. "I kept after him to carve me that head, but he kept putting me off and putting me off," recalls Gene. So rather than rock the boat by continuing to nag, Gene decided to try it herself. Joe made her a "rough out," which is a block of wood that's been crudely cut for carving, and by trial and error, Gene whittled the Santa she wanted.

That was 1988. Gene and Joe had retired together five years earlier, having worked for years at the same coal company—Joe as the machine shop foreman and Gene in the accounts payable department. The couple began attending monthly meetings of the Tri-State Wood Carvers in nearby Evansville, Indiana. Gene took a few classes from a local carver and the couple began showing their work at carving shows. Joe concentrates on the Western figures he favors, and Gene makes nothing but Santas. And both are very happy.

AN UNUSUAL NAME

As for Gene's unusual name, she freely admits it was a mistake. When she was born, the doctor accidentally wrote "Gene" on the birth certificate instead of "Jean." The family never picked up the birth certificate, so for the first 17 years of her life, she went by "Jean." When she finally saw her birth certificate as a teenager, she switched the spelling of her name.

WHITTLED AND DRESSED

Gene's Santas have carved faces, mittens, and boots and usually these are whittled from basswood, which grows locally but often is "imported" from Wisconsin and Minnesota. The carved parts are doweled to the body, which is a piece of scrap wood. The arms are fashioned so they move, but the legs are stationary. The figures then are painted and dressed. Gene estimates that it takes her about as long to sew the outfits as it does to do the carving. She has to hunt for just the right scraps of fabric, and just the right accoutrements. Designing clothing is second nature for her, she says.

Right: *Each Santa in this collection carved by Joe Parsons represents a Christmas gift to his wife, Gene.*

"I've always sewn, from the time I was a kid. I took home economics in school, was a 4-H leader, and made most of my girls' clothes."

She also makes carved Santas exclusively from wood with painted outfits instead of fabric ones. Her design inspirations come partly from looking through books but primarily from her imagination. "Sometimes the shape of the wood will suggest something," she says.

Whenever a new creation is finished, like as not, Gene will give it away. The couple has two daughters and a son, six grandchildren, five step-grandchildren, and three great-grandchildren, so there's a ready supply of recipients. She's sold a few of her Santas, and is generous about donating them for fund-raising auctions, but both Gene and Joe prefer to keep their carving a hobby, not a business.

SHARING A CRAFT

They both do carving demonstrations in schools. Joe appreciates the interest and honesty of children. "They'll ask you right out why did you make the face like this or like that," he says.

The couple, who've worked together for so many years, has an ongoing project that's entirely appropriate. They've been carving a Noah's Ark for more than a year. "I don't know if we'll ever get it done," sighs Gene. But they work at it, two by two, just as a Noah would have wanted.✦

This droopy Santa face ornament, about 5 inches long, was carved and painted by Joe.

Opposite: *Audrey Swarz discovered this brass sleigh and reindeer in an antiques shop. She created reins for one of Santa's hands, and for the other she fashioned a leather-covered book that lists "good boys and girls."*

Face Value

ONE LOOK AT THE ENGAGING EXPRESSIONS ON AUDREY SWARZ'S SCULPTED SANTAS AND YOU WILL BELIEVE.

For years, Audrey Swarz was an artist without a medium. She owned a yarn shop with her mother but didn't know how to knit. She tackled an assortment of crafts but never found her niche. And then, 14 years ago, she stumbled upon a gallery in Bloomfield, Michigan, that changed her life.

"I walked into a one-of-a-kind gallery and saw all these little people who I thought could probably breathe, they looked so real," Audrey recalls. "I took my husband back the next day and said to him, 'You have to see these dolls! They're like you and me.' And I knew that if I didn't use this new inspiration to create my own art, I'd just pop!"

For the next two years, Audrey experimented with a variety of media and techniques to create her own sculptures from polymer clay. She readily admits that her earliest efforts were more than a bit disappointing.

"We live on a lake, and there are many fishermen who work on it," Audrey says. "When I would get really fed up with an early sculpture, I'd stand out on our

Written by Debra Solberg Gibson ✦ *Photographs by Perry Struse*

One of Audrey's personal favorites,
this sleepy Santa rests on the head of his elf.

upper balcony and throw the heads into the lake. We always wondered what would happen if the fishermen ever found one!"

"I still have the very first head I ever sculpted—on a stick," Audrey adds with her characteristic laugh. "Now, whenever I'm frustrated with my work, I get him out of the closet and parade him around the house to remind myself where I started."

SANTA IN DETAIL

Where she's ended up is spectacular. Audrey now creates exquisite collectible Santas ranging in size from 18 inches to life-size adult proportions. The intricate details of the faces, in particular, are a trademark of her work, creating a look that's exceptionally lifelike and expressive.

The heads are molded onto an aluminum-foil base, and then the heavy clay is built out, adding facial details, wrinkles, and texture. Glass eyes are the finishing touch. The sculptures' bodies are constructed from cloth over wire armatures and then stuffed.

> Often Audrey creates an entire Santa around a single piece of fabric or an inspirational accessory.

The Santas' costumes are yet another hallmark of Audrey's awe-inspiring work. Though she'd never sewn a stitch prior to sculpting Santas, Audrey has constructed remarkable outfits (including handmade leather boots) for all of her creations. She scours shops both locally (she lives, appropriately enough, in Holly, Michigan) and in nearby Detroit for both imported and vintage fabrics and unique embellishments. Often Audrey creates an entire Santa around a single piece of fabric or an inspirational accessory. A workshop Santa, for

Opposite: *This 34-inch Santa is representative of many of Audrey's pieces. A "working" Santa, he wears a vest rather than a jacket and is surrounded by teddy bears, another hallmark of Audrey's work.*

Right: *Audrey's Santas' faces are her trademark. "I may make an entire costume and then start all over if it doesn't fit the face."*

instance, might be clothed in a vest constructed from an antique tapestry, with a blouse made from a vintage petticoat. Another might be swathed in red velvet or in trousers shaped from soft gray flannel. Many of her pieces have been dressed in charming hand-knit sweaters—made, of course, by Audrey herself.

All of Audrey's Santas boast wigs, beards, and eyebrows made from angora mohair. The Toledo, Ohio, native cleans and dyes the mohair and then arranges the thousands of individual strands "the way I want them to curl," spending hours and hours on just one beard, for instance.

That commitment to perfection, coupled with "a mind that never stops," requires an intensive work schedule. Audrey rises at 2 a.m. ("I wake up the birds") and either sculpts or constructs costumes until about 4 in the afternoon. Evenings are spent sketching new ideas.

AN EXPANDING ART

Over time, her art has expanded to include the sculpting of elves, angels and fairies. In addition, she's begun to create life-size figures, including butlers and an elderly ticket taker for a family's home theatre.

Left: These three dolls are dressed in imported silk velvet with embroidered silk trims. The little girl holds an antique doll that Audrey saved for several years, waiting for just the right sculpture.

Opposite: Audrey created this Santa for her brother and his wife, incorporating their home's neutral color scheme. Typical of Audrey's attention to details, the angels' wings are made from real feathers.

Audrey's sculptures can be found in select gift shops across the country, although the bulk of her business is conducted on the Internet. Her Web site is attracting a growing number of fans who appreciate and purchase her work. In fact, Audrey has begun teaching Santa-sculpting classes online.

"I love teaching, and I love seeing people's work evolve," she explains. "Inspiring other artists is such a wonderful outlet for me. Eventually, I'd love to be able to include their creations on my Web site as well."

Meanwhile, Audrey continues to celebrate her love of the Yuletide season

"When I begin a project," Audrey explains, "I let the clay decide what it wants to do. It's still amazing to me how it becomes alive right in front of my eyes. If I see a face that interests me, it will just stick in my head until eventually it comes out in the clay. Because my sculptures are so lifelike, I've had customers tell me they actually startle guests who walk into a room where they're displayed. My own aunt won't sleep in our guest room until we remove all my work!"

through her winsome creations. "When we were growing up, Christmas was huge, with all the traditions," Audrey, who is Jewish, remembers. "Santa was always such a special part of that, representing warmth and giving and love. My dad especially loved Christmas, which meant we had a menorah on the table and a tree in the corner. Now my work can continue that love for the holidays— although mine are probably among the few Santas that have Jewish noses!" ✦

Right: *Last year, Elizabeth broadened her Father Christmas repertoire by designing a Mrs. Claus.*

Opposite: *Ranging in height from 3 to 4 feet tall, each of these Santas has a unique personality.*

In the Details

PERSONAL TOUCHES,
INCLUDING HAND-CARDED
WOOL BEARDS AND HAIR,
DISTINGUISH ELIZABETH
RAOL'S SANTAS.

For Elizabeth Raol of Spokane, Washington, Christmas Past is very much a part of Christmas Present. Her 1913 home, resplendent in the old-world Father Christmas figures she's fashioned for six years, is rich in tradition. And throughout her rooms, here and there are all the handmade ornaments and trims that have been special to her since she was a young child.

Elizabeth's gift-giving figures range in size from 18 inches to 5 feet, and she makes about 36 each year. For many years an artisan who specialized in pottery and tole painting, she's gradually perfected the style of her Father Christmases.

Early on, she created soft-sculpture faces and made the figures stand upright by building them over wine

Continued on page 88

Written by Carol McGarvey ✦ *Photographs by Perry Struse*

Elizabeth Raol custom-dressed the Santa on the left using vintage fabrics. The figures with the fishing pole and walking stick were personalized for her sons.

Left and below: Elizabeth Raol created this 4-foot Santa as a Christmas gift for her daughter. She also sculpts many of the items that go into the basket she attaches to the back of each Santa.

bottles. Now, however, she makes the faces and hands from clay, and the figures have armatures under their robes that makes them appear to be walking.

COLLECTING FOR SANTA

Elizabeth spends hours and hours on the details of each figure, but it's hard to calculate the total time she spends on each one. "I have never worked on just one Santa at a time," she points out. "Instead, I might work on several heads and then several garments."

Often working at her dining-room table throughout the year, Elizabeth utilizes fabrics and trims she collects on her many outings. "I haunt flea markets and vintage clothing stores, looking for just the right pieces in silks, brocades, plaids, leathers, buttons, and fur trims." Depending on the fabric selection, of course, the figures can take on an elegant Victorian look or a woodsy outdoors one.

Each face reflects a different personality by the time Elizabeth completes it, and that determines the type of robe and detailing the figure calls for. She also adds glass eyes to give each character a twinkle all its own.

The crowning glory comes from the snow-white hair and beard, which are hallmarks of Elizabeth's art. She doesn't purchase the wool from a supplier in the usual sense. Instead, she goes right to the source, getting her fleece from an Idaho sheep farmer. She then washes and cards the wool to achieve her signature look.

ADDED TOUCHES

Sometimes Elizabeth does custom orders, incorporating special fabrics or details for clients. "It's very special to see a Father Christmas dressed in the fabric from a

Because the faces are hand-sculpted, each of Elizabeth's Santas is different in character.

great-grandmother's elegant 1800s opera coat," she says. "That way, the fabric is out there for all to see, not tucked away in a trunk in an attic."

However, she emphasizes that sometimes it's difficult to do a custom order because an artist can never be completely sure what a client has in mind.

Elizabeth gets help on making the extras for her figures, such as ski poles and toys, from her husband, Pradyumansinh, a native of India, whom she met in college in her home state of Montana.

He is Hindu, she is Christian, and they raised their four children, now grown, with both traditions. The couple also enjoys the company of four grandchildren.

A LONG TRADITION

It would be impossible to overstate the impact of Christmas on her life. Elizabeth's birth family was steeped in the holiday. There were always cranberries to string, kettles of popcorn to pop, and paper chains to fold. "Making gifts was part of my family's hands-on approach to saving pennies," Elizabeth explains, "My siblings and I still exchange homemade gifts as a way of sharing our talents." Her brother is a master woodcrafter, one sister creates paper collages, and another is a veritable magician at needlework.

Christmas trees at the Raol home sparkle with old-fashioned bubble lights, paper ornaments created by Elizabeth's mother, and a collection of miniature '56 Thunderbirds, special to her car-collector husband.

There are other special holiday remembrances she displays during the holidays—Victorian pop-up books, a candle chandelier from India, Christmas crackers for making noise, and a time-honored crèche from the 1950s. The family's grown children enjoy making jam-filled kolaches (Polish pastries) on Christmas Eve. The holiday treasures come out before Thanksgiving and stay up through Epiphany in early January.

Elizabeth sells her Father Christmas creations at two shows held at her home—one, a Christmas in July sale, and the other, a preholiday event in November. Last year for the first time, she exhibited at Spokane's Junior League show and introduced her figures to an appreciative new audience. She also has a business decorating for weddings, corporate dinners, and various special events in the Spokane area.

Now she's branching out to include a female gift-bearer, La Befana, along with some childlike figures. Creating an innocent look in the children's faces is proof of her talent.

Just as with real children, Elizabeth finds the hardest part is letting go of some of her figures. "I try not to get too attached to them. I want them to go out and give joy to others."

For her, part of that joy is leaving something lasting to others—just as her parents did for her. So, last year, she gave each of her children a Father Christmas for their own homes. ✦

With a collection of close to 4,000 molds, Kathi plans to design Santas for a long time to come. She hopes her children will continue the legacy.

Wonders of Walnut Ridge

FROM MOLD TO MAGNIFICENCE, KATHI LORANCE BEJMA'S REPRODUCTION CHALKWARE SANTAS CAST A SPECIAL GLOW ON OLD ST. NICK.

I f Kathi Lorance Bejma's Santa molds could talk, they'd probably be shouting, "Choose *me*, choose *me!*" Stocked on shelves among 4,000 other antique chocolate molds, these lifeless shapes would be screaming to be picked as next in the ever-expanding line of Walnut Ridge Collectibles.

Of the 60,000 chalkware figurines Kathi produces each year, 40,000 of them are Santas—and every one is meticulously poured, dried, detailed, and finished. Year-round, Santas are introduced and retired, and

each has a special place. With their snow-dusted frames and serious stares, they exude the charm of old-world St. Nick. Long textured beards, fur-trimmed coats, and tiny treasures come to life with acrylic paint that promises to last much longer than German chocolate.

Opposite: *Created from her own collection of antique German chocolate molds, Kathi's stern-faced Belsnickles warn children to be good. Kathi's artist friend painted the Belsnickles in the background, which also are available through Walnut Ridge Collectibles.*

Written by Judith Stern Friedman ✦ Photographs by Perry Struse

At Christmas time, Santas convene on Kathi's mantel. Some are retired, some are current, but Kathi plays no favorites. "I just love the joy they bring," she says.

Late 1800s Anton Reiche molds are highly sought after for their exquisite details. This 24-inch-tall Santa carrying a puppet and sword can take up to two weeks to pour, dry, paint, and finish.

"I get lots of letters from collectors," Kathi says from her Westland, Michigan, manufacturing facility (halfway between Ann Arbor and Detroit). "They tell me how much they love their pieces, how much joy our Santas bring." This connection has driven Kathi to continue spreading the spirit of Santa year-round.

CASTING THE CHARACTERS

"We never do one of anything," Kathi says. "We always have an assembly line." Her company of 30 people—including her daughter and son—occupies 15,000 square feet of space with temperature- and humidity-controlled rooms. Each figurine is made from a special composition Kathi developed. "Antique chalkware is very soft," she explains, "and early pieces are not in good shape." Aiming for a longer-lasting medium, Kathi experimented and gradually created her own secret recipe. Now the company outsources the pouring phase, but the rest of the process happens in-house.

"Each piece is a work of art," Kathi says. Once they're poured and dried, the Santas are carefully unmolded, sanded, and cleaned. "I'm picky about how the faces look," she adds. Kathi personally trains her artists to freehand-paint her designs. "It's very labor-intensive," she adds. Strings of holly, lettering, striping, and miniature snow scenes require skilled hands and a steady brush.

Walnut Ridge Collectibles introduces seven new Santas each year, ranging in size from 2 inches to 3 feet tall and in price from $20 to $700. This 3-foot-tall traditional Santa comes from an early-1900s mold.

Each figure is signed, numbered, and dated, then finished with an antiquing process—accomplished by brushing and hand-rubbing—to give the figures an old-world patina. A specially formulated glitterlike "diamond dust" is added for a final embellishment.

A MAGICAL JOURNEY

Kathi has taken Walnut Ridge Collectibles on a journey she never could have imagined. Disenchanted with the 9-to-5 job world, and with no formal art training, she set out 25 years ago to do something on her own. Under the name Walnut Ridge Primitives—named for the street on which she lived—she began to design crafts for folk art shows. "I also am an avid Santa collector," she adds. "Santa was a very big part of what I did—soft sculpture, wood, you name it." In 1984, she found an antique chocolate mold to add to her collection. "I was going to put it away," she recalls, "but instead I decided to play around with it."

"Playing around" became a serious venture when Kathi took fifteen molded figures to a show and they disappeared immediately. Inspired, she continued to develop the medium, going to shows and searching out sources for more antique molds. In June 1988, she attended her first wholesale show at Valley Forge, Pennsylvania. The first day she wrote $26,000 in orders, and by the end of the show, the total was over $60,000. "It was incredible," Kathi says. "And it was just me."

What started out as a small experiment in Kathi's basement grew into an impressive manufacturing business. By 1990, Kathi had leased a 1,580-square-foot building. "I remember thinking I'm never going to fill this up," she recalls. But within six months she expanded again, and then built the building they occupy now.

Kathi feels fortunate to be working with her children, Jacqueline, 30, and Jeff, 27. Jackie runs the day-to-day activities and Jeff oversees the warehouse and shipping. Meanwhile, Kathi pursues her greatest joys: designing Santas and attending trade shows. "I've developed wonderful friendships with my customers," she says fondly.

As she surveys her molds for the next release, Kathi deliberates over every detail. "Choose *me!* Choose *me!*" the Santas seem to scream. It's the lucky one who comes to life in Kathi's loving hands.◆

Opposite: *Snow-white Santas, fresh from their molds, wait in lines to be painted by Walnut Ridge Collectibles artists. For consistency, each painter works on the same figurine model, painting the details repeatedly. When completed, each Santa will get a handrubbed coat of antiquing medium and a sprinkling of special glitter before heading to a store and its eventual home.*

Opposite: *A resin Santa holding a
lantern is titled "Where's Rudolph." In
front of the Santa is one of Pipka's
glass ball ornaments, called kugels.*

Santa's Student

PIPKA ULVILDEN'S INTERNATIONAL SANTAS HAVE
AMAZING CULTURAL DETAIL. NO WONDER! HER RESEARCH
INCLUDES SPENDING CHRISTMAS ABROAD.

S anta designer Pipka Ulvilden is nothing if not
international in her outlook. Born in
Czechoslovakia to a Czech-Hungarian father and
German mother and raised in the United States, Pipka
has spent decades studying how countries around the
world celebrate Christmas. She has literally hundreds
of books on the subject, enough to fill one wall of
shelves in both her Sister Bay, Wisconsin, summer
home and her Florida winter home.

And it's not unusual at all for her to spend Christmas
abroad—in the Netherlands, Switzerland, or the
Caribbean—to see firsthand how different cultures
celebrate the season.

"You can read all the books in the world," she says,
"but it is very different to be there and absorb the
atmosphere. Oftentimes, I'll see one little detail that I've
overlooked before and it makes all the difference."

"People everywhere
are drawn to Santa."

Written by Allison Engel ✦ Photographs by Perry Struse

DIFFERENT, YET THE SAME

Thanks to her on-site research, she's designed an Australian Santa with a sleigh pulled by "boomers" (kangaroos) and a Polish Santa wearing a villager's sheepskin coat trimmed with a traditional embroidered braid. A Caribbean Santa carries a broom and a soft woven basket on his back to hold white sand from the beach. A Caribbean tradition is to pour sand around your home, sweep designs into it, and line the sand with conch shells.

Santas everywhere are united in purpose, to bring peace and goodwill to all, Pipka believes. "Santa is a deeply spiritual figure to me," she says earnestly. "All around the world there are Santas, and no one ever fights or argues that my Santa is the only one or the best one, as happens with religion. Everyone accepts him and accepts each other's Santa. People everywhere are drawn to Santa."

Above and opposite: *Pipka's Caribbean Santa has a green robe, a conch shell at his ear, and a broom for sweeping white sand into festive designs.*

Below: *Though Pipka first gained fame as a painter, her three-dimensional resin Santas are now highly collectible.*

Opposite: *Painted wood international Santas, including an Australian Santa and kangaroo at* top right, *line the stairs at Pipka's gallery in Wisconsin.*

THE NEWEST SUCCESS

Pipka has been designing Santa figures for Prism, a company based in Manhattan, Kansas, for seven years, and her resin figures have become highly collectible. When new, they are modestly priced at $95 to $120 for the 11-inch-tall limited-edition Santas and $40 for the 6-inch Santas that are produced in greater numbers. On the secondary market, however, prices have skyrocketed. A Czech Santa with a black embroidered coat that she designed in her first year of production for Prism now sells for $3,000 to $5,000—if you can find one.

A MODEST BEGINNING

Although collectors around the world eagerly await her next Santas, Pipka started out very modestly, learning about decorative painting the hard way. In 1972, as a single mother with two children under the age of five, she started a business in Minneapolis— Pipka's Workshop—where she scrounged old trunks and chairs at garage sales and on street corners and painted them in Bavarian designs. This free-style folk art, emphasizing florals, pictorial scenes, sayings, and prayers, was something she'd seen as a child in Czechoslovakia.

Pipka is entirely self-taught, and has always relied on her own ingenuity to get the business started. "I did it totally out of passion and thinking this would be a way to provide for my family," she says. "It turned out to be a great education, particularly when customers brought

Because Pipka has always painted Santas whose backs are as detailed as the fronts, they're natural subjects for three-dimensional figurines.

in pieces for me to do custom painting. I learned all about combining different colors that I never would have used."

A NEW LIFE

After 13 years of running Pipka's Workshop, she remarried, moved to Sister Bay, Wisconsin, and opened

Pipka's Gallery and Gifts, selling her own hand-painted items as well as giftware by other folk artists. Realizing that she could paint only so many items in a day, she turned to creating designs that could be reproduced in limited editions. She sent portfolios to several companies and went with a start-up firm, Prism, run by Michele Johnson and Gary Meidinger, who mortgaged their homes and cashed in their pension plans to get the business started. Their determination to make Prism a success was something Pipka could relate to, having done the same thing herself years earlier.

Pipka's collectible figures are made of cold-cast resin that includes marble and porcelain, contributing to their heavy and substantial feel. Pipka draws the designs on flat art boards, which are sent to a master sculptor in Taiwan, who turns them into three-dimensional clay figures. After molds are made, the figures are cast in China, where every joint is meticulously hand-sanded and the figures are painted. At every step, Pipka sees prototypes and often makes changes until she's completely satisfied.

Pipka also has licensed her designs to the Kalaidoscope Company, which puts them on handblown glass balls that are painted in Poland. In European tradition, kugels are hung on velvet or satin ribbons from a chandelier or in another place of honor. "They aren't designed to fill up a tree," explains Pipka. "They are treated as individual works of art."

Pipka also designs angels and Madonna figures, which she finds as rewarding as her Santa designs. She remarks, "There isn't anything about my job that isn't uplifting. I'm on my knees in thanks every day."✦

Above: *Pipka's resin Santas have amazing detail.*

Left: *The kugel ornaments Pipka designs are hand-painted in Poland.*

Pipka designs Santas in many forms and sizes. Compare the large three-dimensional Santa at center front with the painted one to its right.

"You always have to be coming up with different ideas to keep it fun," Susan says. Instead of sculpting the beards, she glued wool and mohair onto these burly papier-mâché Santas.

An Elf in Disguise

IN THE REMOTE INDIANA
COUNTRYSIDE, WHERE ARCTIC
WINTER WINDS BLOW,
ONE BUSY SUSAN BRACK
IS DRAWING, SCULPTING, SEWING,
AND SMILING—ALL FOR THE
LOVE OF SANTA.

At daybreak in the small town of Liberty, Indiana, on a small farm, in a busy kitchen, Susan Brack is stirring up another batch of papier-mâché. She'll load a line of idle molds then carry them out to the deep freeze on the porch. Days, weeks, and sometimes months later, the soggy forms evolve into Santas that capture a bit of Christmas magic.

In another room, Susan picks up a pencil to sketch the snow scene she dreamed about last night. Or maybe she'll stencil the fabric St. Nick that will be this year's collectible release. Dabbling in many crafts—and accomplished at all—Susan Brack is a sprightly soul whose passion for Christmas has become her career.

Written by Judith Stern Friedman ✦ *Photographs by Craig Anderson*

Most of Susan's ideas originate with her illustrations—a masterful blend of colored pencil and watercolors. Each piece of art is then reproduced for different lines.

She creates such a large sampling of Santas in so many different shapes and sizes that they barely fit on the shelves of her mother's shop, The Enchanted Sleigh, in nearby Centerville, Indiana. Stocking more than 100 handmade pieces year-round, the shop is Susan's primary retail outlet, though much of her work also is sold through other venues. As Christmas cards, collectible figurines, rub-on transfers, and cross-stitch samplers, her designs transcend all media.

MAGIC IN MOTION

"Illustration is my first love," Susan says. "Ever since I was little, I loved to draw. That's a gift I have." Inspired by her collection of vintage Christmas decorations, Susan allows her ideas to guide her. Diversity keeps her projects fresh and interesting. "As soon as it becomes work, I quit," she explains. "Once I get tired of drawing, I totally change direction and move on to other projects."

Her papier-mâché figures—formed from her antique confectionery molds—are time-intensive creations. They require a complicated layering process that often forms air bubbles that cause parts to collapse. "It's tricky," Susan explains. After years of experimenting, she eventually developed an instinct for how to do it. On more delicate pieces, she inserts wire or toothpicks to prevent breakage. "Some still don't make it through the process," she says. In any one day, she'll make as many as 25 figures that involve long drying periods, careful patching, and meticulous painting.

When she's not pouring molded figures, Susan pours out other creations, such as sculpted clay Santa faces with fabric bodies. "I'll do something totally different from one year to the next," Susan says. Since 1986, she's taught quilting and stenciling classes, which

To look at the works of art in her home, and to see her unequivocal craftsmanship, one might mistake Susan Brack for a Christmas elf.

Above: *Pressed papier-mâché is Susan's labor-intensive technique for creating Santas from antique chocolate molds. "It's taken me several years to get the right kind of texture," she says.*

Right: *Vintage rag dolls inspired Susan to sew this primitive-looking Santa. He sports antique fabrics and buttons from a friend, a baked-clay face, and a mohair beard.*

also influence her Santa creations. Some loyal customers anticipate stenciled fabric Santas, such as the boldly dressed figures on *pages 110–111.* Susan's fondness for Fruit Stripe gum inspired the crafty-looking character in the striped suit.

The customer base for her handmade pieces is primarily local, as Susan sells them only through The

Above: *These three-dimensional "Stars and Stripes" figures, all with patriotic socks, were created from one of Susan's illustrations and are sold nationwide by Gallerie II.*

Left: *Hand-sculpted, one-of-a-kind Santas like these are increasingly difficult for Susan to produce because of other demands. They sell for $30 to $300, depending on size and detailing.*

Enchanted Sleigh; however, the shop's location on a major highway does draw tourists. Susan says she's learned that everybody has different tastes. "Just because I don't like something," she explains, "chances are somebody will. Some customers like very simple pieces, and others love sparkly or textured things."

HANDMADE, HEARTFELT

Susan makes all of her Santas single-handedly; yet her occupation has become a family affair. She began in 1986, when her children were young, searching for a way to earn money. "I started going to crafts shows with teddy bears, Santas, and oil paintings," she recalls. "As I became successful at the bigger shows, I found I didn't like traveling." In 1988, she opened The

"I tend to incorporate fantasy into my Santas."

Reflecting Susan's quilting background, these stenciled fabric Santa dolls are collectors' items. Susan manufactures a limited number of signed-and-dated designs each year.

Enchanted Sleigh, a one-room shop out of her home, with one corner devoted exclusively to her crafts.

Susan's mother, Norma Jones, aunt Nancy Smith, and uncle Jerry Stone filled the rest of the room with antiques, while her sister, Connie Toschlog, a folk artist, contributed other hand-sculpted items. Her daughter, Rachel, now a fine artist in New York, also contributed some designs.

By 1998, Susan's work had grown to the point that she turned the shop over to her mother when they relocated it to its more visible Centerville address. "I just wanted to do my art," Susan says, although she still regularly sends new Santas to the shop. As a freelance artist, she works directly with an agent, who keeps her busy developing new product.

"I've always loved the old German expressions," Susan explains. "I tend to incorporate fantasy into my Santas." Now she's sharing those fantasies with the rest of the world. "Santa can be so many different things to different people," she adds. As she sits back, content to continue crafting, one wonders what surprises she'll dream up next.✦

Try making a Santa designed by Susan and her daughter, Rachel, with instructions on page 139.

*Kathy showed her creativity early —
by age 9, she was sewing all
her own clothes.*

Everything New
Is Old Again

CANADIAN ARTIST
KATHY PATTERSON
CAME UP WITH AN INGENIOUS
SOLUTION TO ACQUIRING
ANTIQUE SANTAS —
SHE CREATES HER OWN.

Kathy Patterson's childhood holiday memories are filled with countless visits to her grandmother's festive home. There, the colorful lights, sparkling ornaments, and miniature teapots scattered throughout the house intrigued Kathy. But she was most drawn to the mantel lined with antique German Santas.

As an adult, when Kathy began buying her own vintage Santas, she became frustrated by both their scarcity and their cost. One day, as she was inspecting a new purchase, it occurred to her that she could reproduce the look herself.

Opposite: *These samples of Kathy's 2001 collection include two 34-inch candy containers, similar to what may have been found long ago on the counters of German general stores or butcher shops.*

Written by Debra Solberg Gibson ✦ *Photographs by Perry Struse*

"What I wanted to re-create was the look I remembered from going to Nana's when I was little," Kathy explains. "When you collect something, you tend to get addicted to it, and then you become a collector who has to get better and better pieces."

It was Kathy's belief that the best pieces could come right from her own hands. She began making molds from the German Santas she'd collected, most of which were candy containers. The dolls are made from a mixture of gypsum, papier-mâché, and polymer, resulting in pieces that are very light, thin, and strong. The Santas

One of Kathy's new series features Santas riding animals. The cart pulled by the pig serves as a candy container. Both the Santa riding the cloth-covered bear and the one on the reindeer are pull toys.

range in size from 5 to 34 inches. The cylinders that are inserted into them generally are made of cardboard.

The original Santas made in Germany prior to World War I were produced by cottage industries operated primarily in homes. "Their [the Germans'] molds were their most prized possessions," Kathy explains, "because that was their livelihood."

There are many steps in Kathy's reproduction process. Shelves in Kathy's studio are lined with dozens of papier-mâché heads and boots, below. *When the painting and assembly have been completed,* above, *she turns to her huge stash of materials,* right.

AN AUTHENTIC CHALLENGE

Those original creations, however, were hastily made. The materials were very inferior, with horsehair often imbedded into the papier-mâché. The Santas' costumes were constructed from thin, inexpensive fabrics. It was these very imperfections that have proved to be the greatest challenges in reproducing the pieces.

"The first Santas I made didn't look anything like the old ones," Kathy remembers. "The originals were painted very quickly, and often the eyes didn't even match. It was awkward for me to put myself into the frame of mind to reproduce these pieces authentically, because I wanted to make them more perfect. I had to work hard to lose that. To more accurately reproduce the original look, I began to paint faster. Now I paint an eye in a minute instead of an hour."

Many of Kathy's Santas carry baskets that are handwoven, some by an 80-year-old man still living in a German village who has been weaving baskets since he was eight.

Opposite: These Santas range in size from 5 to 19 inches and feature handblown miniature glass icicles in their beards.

Likewise, creating costumes for the Santas requires scavenging for low-quality fabrics (primarily flannels, felts, and woolens) made from natural fibers that may even be considered "seconds" by their manufacturers. For additional authenticity, Kathy hand-dyes all her fabrics, mostly to achieve a mottled appearance.

Though Kathy is diligent about conserving these age-authentic details, she's equally forthcoming about her Santas' origins to their potential purchasers.

"I'm not trying to trick anybody," she says. "There are plenty of telltale signs that my Santas are re-creations. For instance, a specific kind of cardboard was used originally for the inside cylinder, but I use a 25-mm chipboard that is made today. I used to look for old wood for the Santas' bases, but now I use new wood. I also stamp my initials on the pieces, as well as the date I made them."

Though Kathy has never received any formal art training, her technique defies even her most valiant attempts to duplicate an original. "I have a much finer, longer brushstroke than the early Germans," she explains.

"My painting is my signature—it's like comparing beautiful handwriting to backhand penmanship. As much as I try to simply copy their work, I always incorporate my own style into it."

Kathy continues to enjoy the self-imposed task of "trying to make them better all the time, and more believable, but I'm still not all the way there," she says.

THE HUNT

Equally challenging is her ongoing quest to find high-quality original German Santas to replicate. "There's a lot of just average stuff out there," she says, "and the people I make these Santas for don't want 'average.' They want what they can't find." Consequently, Kathy attends annual Golden Glow of Christmas Past conventions to seek out originals. She also buys them from private collectors and depends on friends who travel each year to Germany to scout the countryside for the rare pieces.

Her favorite reproduction to date is a 34-inch candy container in the shape of a standing Santa. "He has a really wonderful face," Kathy explains. "A lot of the German Santa faces are very average-looking, but he has a very different and beautiful face. I like to paint those."

Her most challenging project to date? A 20-inch "nodder," a Santa whose head is counterbalanced on wire so when it's touched, it nods back and forth. "With nodders, you have to be sure that the papier-mâché you pour will end up weighting properly, or the head won't nod," she explains.

Kathy's future plans include adding more studio space to the rural Paris, Ontario, home she shares with her husband, Helmut, and their two children (coincidentally named Holly and Nick). She also hopes "to try each year to do something different than the last year. I'll keep looking for more unusual pieces to copy. As long as I'm still challenged to make the Santas and I continue to find pieces that challenge me, that's what I'll be doing." ✦

PERSONAL EXPRESSIONS

When you craft a Santa
for your home or as a gift,
you become part of the spirit
of Saint Nicholas—
a tradition that spans more
than 16 centuries.

*Old meets new when photocopying technology
transforms antique postcards into center patches
for crazy-quilt squares.*
—Photograph by Craig Anderson

Santa's Gifts

Finished piece is 13" tall.   *Designed by Dana Thompson*
Photograph by Craig Anderson

MATERIALS

- 12 tea bags
- 2 quarts boiling water
- ½ yard off-white 36"- or 72"-wide wool felt or needled cotton batting
- ¼ yard 44"-wide unbleached muslin
- ⅛ yard 36"-wide wool batting
- Lace-trimmed handkerchief or 7×8" piece of batiste or other lightweight fabric and ¼ yard of ½"-wide lace trim
- Polyester fiberfill
- Sewing thread
- 4 pipe cleaners
- 4—½"-diameter buttons
- Acrylic paints: antique white, blue, brown, gold, and berry
- ½" flat and fine liner brushes
- Black Pigma marker
- Blush
- Crafts glue
- Glitter
- Curly wool
- Thin sturdy cardboard
- Crafts knife, ruler, and cutting mat
- Masking tape
- Gesso
- Snow-Tex or other decorative snow
- Hot glue gun and glue sticks
- ½×6×8" piece of wood
- 12" length of ⅜" wooden dowel
- Drill with assorted bits
- Purchased miniature tree
- Purchased miniature wagon
- Wire

CUT THE FABRICS

Trace the patterns, *pages 124–125,* and cut out. Cut a 9" muslin square and fold in half. On the doubled muslin, trace around the Santa body and the doll body, but *do not* cut out. Set the tracings aside. From the remaining muslin, cut a 1×4" casing strip for Santa and two 1½" squares for the doll arms.

Cut two 4×18" rectangles from the wool felt. Fold each in half lengthwise and finger-press the crease. Placing one edge of the pattern on the crease, trace two arms on one folded rectangle (see Diagram 1) and two legs on the other, but *do not* cut out. Set the tracings aside. From the remaining wool

GENERAL DIRECTIONS

All seam allowances are ¼" *except* on the traced pattern pieces. Use a hot glue gun to secure the pieces together unless otherwise specified.

PREPARE THE FABRICS

Place the tea bags in a large container and pour boiling water over them. Allow to steep for about 5 minutes. Remove the tea bags and gently immerse the wool felt or cotton batting, muslin, wool batting, and handkerchief or batiste and lace trim. Let stand for 20 minutes without agitating or stirring. Squeeze water out of the wool felt and place in the dryer for about 35 minutes. Then lay the wool felt flat and smooth to finish drying. Meanwhile, lay the other fabrics flat to dry.

Diagram 1

Made from wool felt and batting,
this old-fashioned gift-giver, surrounded
by toys of a bygone era, requires only simple
sewing skills. Designer Dana Thompson
suggests you start by giving the fabrics a
hot tea-dye bath to color them and texturize
the wool felt.

felt, use the pattern pieces to cut two coats, two capes, and one hat. From the wool batting, cut a 1×20" strip for the cape trim and a 1×13" strip for the coat-hem trim.

From the handkerchief or batiste, cut a 7×8" rectangle with the handkerchief trim along the 8" edge.

SEW THE SANTA

Sew around the Santa body on the traced outline through both layers of muslin, leaving an opening at the bottom. Trim ¼" from the seams. Clip the curves at the neck and turn right side out. Fold under the edges of the 1×4" muslin strip a scant ¼". Position it on the back of the Santa body with one short edge just below the neck. Carefully slip-stitch the two long edges and the top short edge to the back *only.* Stuff the Santa body with polyester fiberfill. Turn the bottom edges under ¼" and slip-stitch the opening closed.

Sew and cut out the arms and legs in the same manner and turn. Fold the pipe cleaners in half, and insert the folded end of one into each leg and arm. Very lightly stuff close to the top. Turn the top edges of the limbs under ¼" and slip-stitch the openings closed. With the seam centered in the back, bend the bottoms of the legs to create feet. Stitch the legs and arms to the body, with the seams to the back.

Cut one of the coat pieces along the fold line to make two fronts. Sew the fronts to the back. Lightly press the seams open, and turn the coat right side out. Referring to Diagram 2, *above,* glue one long edge of the coat-hem strip to the bottom of the

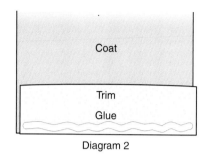

Diagram 2

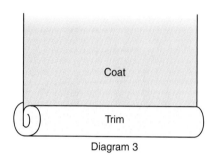

Diagram 3

coat. Roll the remaining long edge to the back (see Diagram 3) and glue in place.

Trim off the extra batting at the front edges. Put the coat on the doll. Lap the left front over the right and glue the top of the coat together. Stitch four small buttons to the coat.

Cut one of the cape pieces along the fold line to make two fronts. Sew the fronts to the back. Lightly press the seams open and turn the cape right side out. Apply the cape trim to the bottom edge in the same manner as for the coat. Place the cape on Santa and stitch together at the center front, about halfway down.

Without unfolding the hat, sew along the seam line (the center back). Hand-sew gathering stitches around the face opening. Place the hat on the doll, adjust the gathers around the face, and slip-stitch the hat to the neck of the coat. Don't secure the face edge yet.

Transfer the facial details from the pattern, *page 125.* Paint antique white

eyes and eyebrows; let dry. Paint the irises blue; dot black centers on the eyes. Use a black Pigma pen to draw the nose and outline the eyes. Blush the cheeks. Glue on curly wool for Santa's beard, mustache, and bangs. Glue the front edge of the hood over the bangs. Thin crafts glue with water and brush it on Santa's shoulders and head. Sprinkle with glitter.

MAKE THE DOLL

Sew around the doll body on the traced line through both layers of muslin, leaving the bottom open. Trim ¼" from the seams. Clip the curves at the neck and turn right side out. Stuff the doll body with polyester fiberfill. Turn the bottom edges under ¼" and slip-stitch the opening closed.

For the batiste dress, turn under one 8" edge of the 7×8" rectangle and stitch on the lace trim. Sew the 7" edges of the handkerchief or batiste rectangle together to form a tube. Turn the remaining 8" edge under ¼" and hand-sew gathering stitches around it for the neck opening. Place on the doll and draw up the stitching and tie off.

Fold one edge of each 1½" square under ¼". Beginning at the opposite edge, roll the remaining fabric into a tube and slip-stitch the folded edge to the roll, tucking the raw edges at one end inside the roll for a hand. Position the arms on the doll and stitch in place, pulling some of the dress fabric around over the shoulder.

Transfer the facial details from the pattern, *page 125,* to the doll's head. Paint the hair brown. Use the black Pigma pen to draw the nose and eyes. Paint on a little berry mouth and gold eyebrows. Blush the cheeks. Bend Santa's arms to the desired positions. Glue the doll in the Santa's right arm.

COMPLETE THE HOUSE AND WAGON

Transfer the house and roof patterns onto sturdy cardboard. Cut each piece using the crafts knife, cutting mat, and ruler. Use the knife to score the roof, side walls, and floor. Fold each piece on the scored lines. Align the open edges of the house and join them with a strip of masking tape the length of the seam. Glue the roof on the house. Apply masking tape over the glued seams. Paint the house, roof, and wagon (except the wheels) with two or three coats of gesso, letting each coat dry. Paint the windows and door of the house gold. When the paint is dry, use the Pigma marker to draw the window-panes. Paint the house and wagon

House
Cut 1

Score and fold

Score and fold

Score and fold

Score and fold

Roof
Cut 1

Score and fold

with a mixture of equal parts of antique white paint with Snow-Tex, overlapping the edges of the windows and door slightly. *Do not* apply the mixture to the bottom of the house. While the snow mixture is still wet, sprinkle on glitter.

ASSEMBLE THE SCENE

Arrange the Santa, house, wagon and tree on the wooden base. Mark positions and drill one hole for the dowel to hold the Santa, the two holes for each of the wagon's front wheels, and the tree. Slip one end of the dowel into the casement on Santa's back. If necessary, trim the dowel so Santa's feet just touch the base. Remove the Santa, and glue the dowel into the base. Wire the wagon in place. Glue the house and tree in place. Apply Snow-Tex and glitter to the base. Place Santa on the dowel.

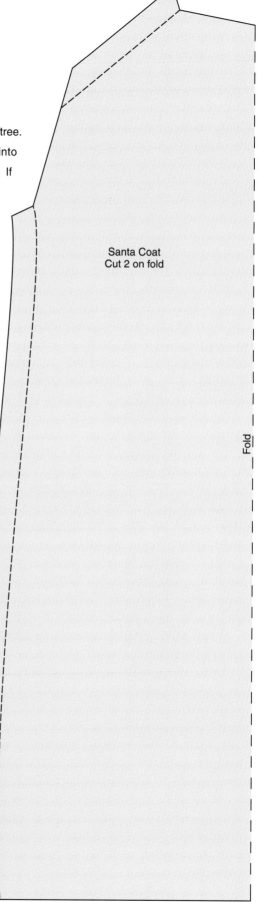

Santa Coat
Cut 2 on fold

Fold

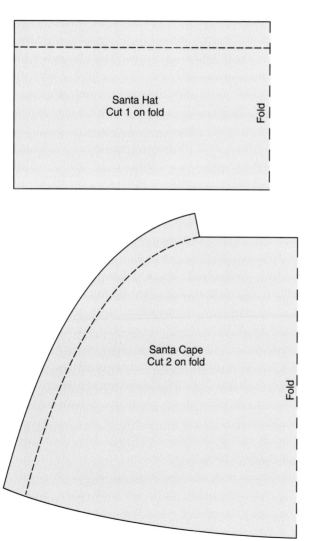

Santa Hat
Cut 1 on fold

Fold

Santa Cape
Cut 2 on fold

Fold

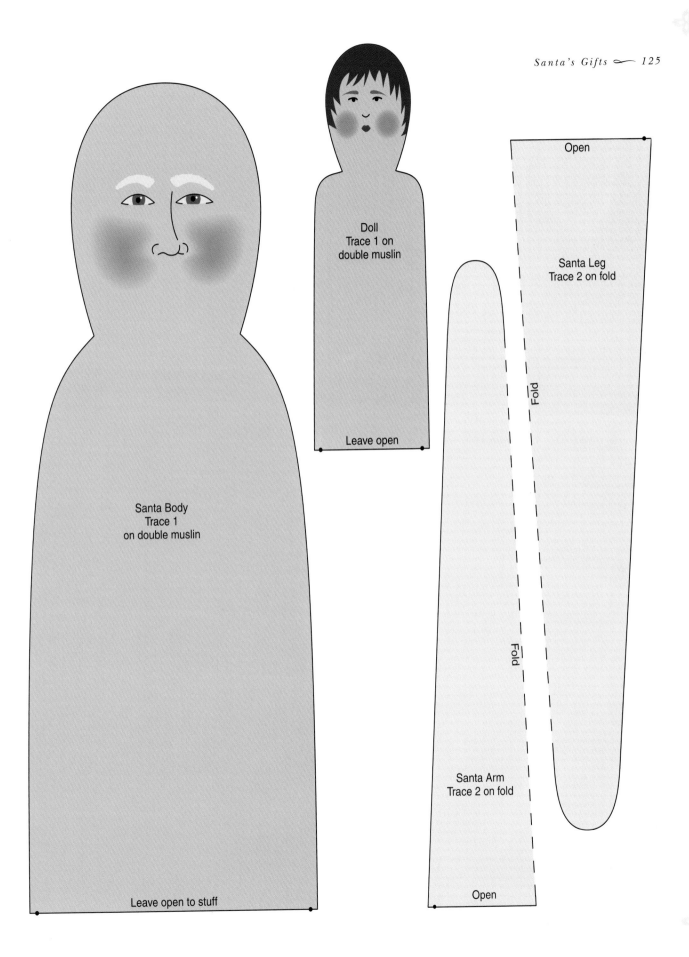

Doll
Trace 1 on
double muslin

Leave open

Santa Body
Trace 1
on double muslin

Leave open to stuff

Open

Santa Leg
Trace 2 on fold

Fold

Fold

Santa Arm
Trace 2 on fold

Open

Santa in Checks

The finished piece is 12½×14½". ✦ *Designed by Mary Jane Todd*
Photographs by Craig Anderson

MATERIALS

- 12½×14½" wooden box with flared sides
- 100- and 150-grit sandpaper
- Wood sealer
- DecoArt Americana Colors: BK Buttermilk (DA3), AW Antique White (DA 58), CN Cool Neutral (DA89), FT Flesh Tone (DA78), SF Shading Flesh (DA137), BF Blush Flesh (DA110), CR Country Red (DA18), CO Cadmium Orange (DA14), NP Napa Red (DA165), BS Burnt Sienna (DA63), PP Plantation Pine (DA113), LB Lamp Black (DA67)
- Brushes: #12 flat, #8 flat, #4 flat, ⅜" angular shaders, ¼" angular shaders, #1 liner
- Chalk pencil
- Antiquing medium
- Clear acrylic varnish

On the wall or as a one-of-a-kind serving piece, Mary Jane Todd's Santa is perfect for the Christmas season. The prefinished box has a flared shape that gives the appearance of extra depth.

GENERAL INSTRUCTIONS

Sand all surfaces, first with 100-, then 150-grit sandpaper. Wipe clean. Seal the wood with wood sealer, and when dry, again sand lightly with the 150-grit sandpaper and wipe clean.

Base-coat with the #12, #8, and #4 brushes, and float shading and highlighting with the ⅜" and ¼" angular shaders, choosing the size that best fits the area. Use the #1 liner to apply the details.

PAINT THE SANTA

Base-coat the entire box, inside and out, with two coats of PP, allowing the paint to dry between coats. In the area behind Santa, paint a stripe of NP, highlighted in the corners with CO.

Transfer the main pattern lines for Santa's face, *page 128*. With FT, base-coat the face and let it dry. Transfer the facial details. Repaint the face and, working wet into wet, shade around the eyes and down the nose on each side with SF and BF. With BS, paint the eyes. With LB, paint the pupils, with BK highlight the BS and put a dot on upper right side of each pupil. With BK, paint the whites of the eyes. With LB, draw a thin line above each eye. Highlight the eyelids with BK.

With CN base-coat the hair, beard, and mustache. Paint the mouth with NP, and highlight the lip area with CO. Paint the cap with CR. Shade with NP, and highlight with CO. Base-coat the pom-pom with CN and highlight with BK. With BK, overstroke the beard, mustache, and hair.

With PP, paint the holly leaves. Highlight with a tiny bit of BK. Paint the berries with NP, and highlight with CO. Add a final highlight of BK.

PAINT THE FRAME

Using the pattern on *page 129* as a guide, use a chalk pencil to mark off the frame edges evenly. With the liner brush and AW draw a line for each square. Fill in alternating squares with AW. Paint the edges of the frame with NP.

Antique, using your favorite method. Let dry and varnish.✦

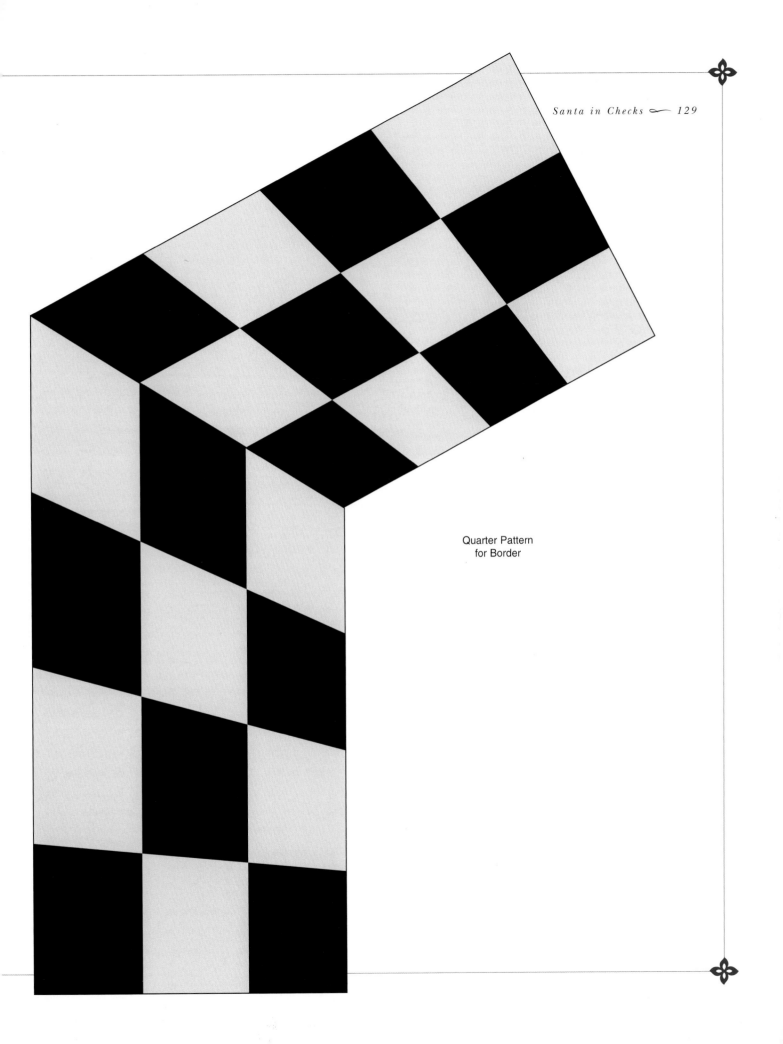

Quarter Pattern
for Border

Nelda Rice has won numerous contest awards for her painted holiday pieces because of the surprising details she adds. This elegant Santa's outstretched hand features a peg to display your favorite bauble.

Santa in White

The finished piece is 17" tall. ✦ *Designed by Nelda Rice*
Photographs by Craig Anderson

MATERIALS

- ½×14×17" pine
- ¾×14×4½" pine
- 100- and 150-grit sandpaper
- Tack cloth
- Three ¾" lengths of ¼" dowel
- ⅝" length of ⅛" dowel
- Wood sealer
- Drill with ⅛" and ¼" bits
- Krylon #1311 Matte Finish
- Woodworker's glue
- Delta Ceramcoat Acrylic Colors: AC Flesh (AF) 2085, Barn Red (BR) 2490, Black 2506, Black Green (BG) 2116, Burnt Umber (BU) 2025, Dark Flesh (DF) 2127, Fleshtone Base (FL) 2082, Hunter Green (HG) 2471, Leaf Green (LG) 2067, Light Ivory (LI) 2401, Peachy Keen (PK) 2555, Persimmon (PE) 2480, Sonoma Wine (SW) 2446, Trail Tan (TR) 2435
- Delta Ceramcoat Gleams: Bronze 2606
- Brushes: #12 synthetic flat, #8 synthetic flat, #4 synthetic flat, #1 synthetic liner, ⅜" synthetic angular shader, ¼" synthetic angular shader, #2 stencil brush, scruffy #6 flat brush

CUT THE WOOD

Transfer the outline for the Santa and his bag onto ½" pine and the base outline onto ¾" pine. Cut out the pieces with a scrollsaw, using a #5R blade. To do the inside cut as shown, follow the scrollsaw manufacturer's instructions. Drill three evenly spaced ¼" holes in the bottom edge of the Santa and three corresponding holes in the base. Drill a ⅛" hole in the mitten as shown on the pattern.

GENERAL INSTRUCTIONS

Sand both pieces on all sides with 100-, then 150-grit sandpaper. Wipe with a tack cloth. Seal the wood with wood sealer, and when it's dry, sand lightly again with the 150-grit sandpaper and wipe clean.

Transfer the main pattern lines to the Santa and bag. There's no need to transfer details—you'll just paint over them. Referring to the photograph on *page 132*, continue the pattern lines onto the sides of the board and onto the back of the Santa and bag.

Base-coat with the #12, #8, and #4 flat brushes, and float shading and highlighting with the ⅜" and ¼" angular shaders, choosing the size that best fits the area. Use the #1 liner to apply details, the #2 stencil brush for stippling, and the scruffy flat brush for dry-brushing highlights.

PAINT SANTA

Base-coat the face PK, the inside of the mouth Black, and the lip PE. Transfer the facial features to the face. Float DF shading under the hat, under the eyebrows, and on each side of the nose. Base-coat the eyebrows AF. When the brows are dry, with LI, start at the outside edge of each one, and add short, overlapping hairlike lines to indicate eyebrows. Work forward to the inside of each brow. Thin DF to ink consistency, and finely line the nose, continuing the line up over the eyes, as shown. Base-coat the whites of the eyes LI and the irises HG. Highlight the lower third of each eye with a float of LG, and when dry, highlight each eye with a dot of LI.

Outline the top of each eye with Black, thinned to ink consistency, then use the thinned paint to make fine, short eyelashes

The painting on the back of Santa in White is a continuation of that on the front.

Base-coat Santa's belt BU, then shade it with BU and Black mixed 1:1. Highlight by dry-brushing with TR.

Base-coat all the fur TR. When the paint is dry, stipple the fur LI, using the #2 stencil brush. Allow the stippling to cover the defined edges of the TR base coat. Base-coat the belt buckle Bronze. Shade the fur TR.

Thin LI to ink consistency, and starting at the bottom of the beard, use the liner to make hairlike lines in the beard. Line the mustache in the same way, and allow the ends of the mustache to blend into the beard. Shade the beard and mustache with AF.

Base-coat the top and bottom of the base piece with LI. When the paint is dry, base-coat the sides of the base AF.

ASSEMBLE THE SANTA

Use woodworker's glue to glue the three ¼"-diameter dowels into the three holes in the bottom of the Santa. Carefully sand the paint off the base where the Santa will be attached. With woodworker's glue, insert the Santa dowels into the base holes. With woodworker's glue, insert the ⅛" dowel into Santa's right mitten. Allow the glue to dry thoroughly. Spray all sides of the piece with Krylon #1311 Matte Finish. ✦

as shown. Float PE on the lower part of the cheeks for blush. When this is dry, over-float very lightly with BR. Dry-brush LI on the apples of the cheeks. Float shading on the corners of the lip with BR, and highlight the center of the lip LI. Base-coat the mustache and beard AF.

Base-coat the bag BR; float shading with SW. When dry, float highlights of PE on the opening edges. Dry-brush additional PE highlights as shown. Apply the pulled-out-dot stars with Bronze.

Base-coat the ⅛"-diameter dowel and the mittens with HG, and float shading on

the mittens with BG. When the paint is dry, highlight by dry-brushing LG. Thin TR to ink consistency and apply the wiggly-line design to the mittens.

Base-coat Santa's hat and robe FL. When the paint is dry, lightly transfer the pattern for the gathers and folds, continuing them onto the back. Line and float the shading on the robe and the hat with TR. Dry-brush highlights of LI. Transfer the pattern for the wavy line of the design on the robe, continuing it onto the sides and back. With slightly thinned HG, line the wavy line and freehand-paint the leaf shapes. Use BR to dot the berries.

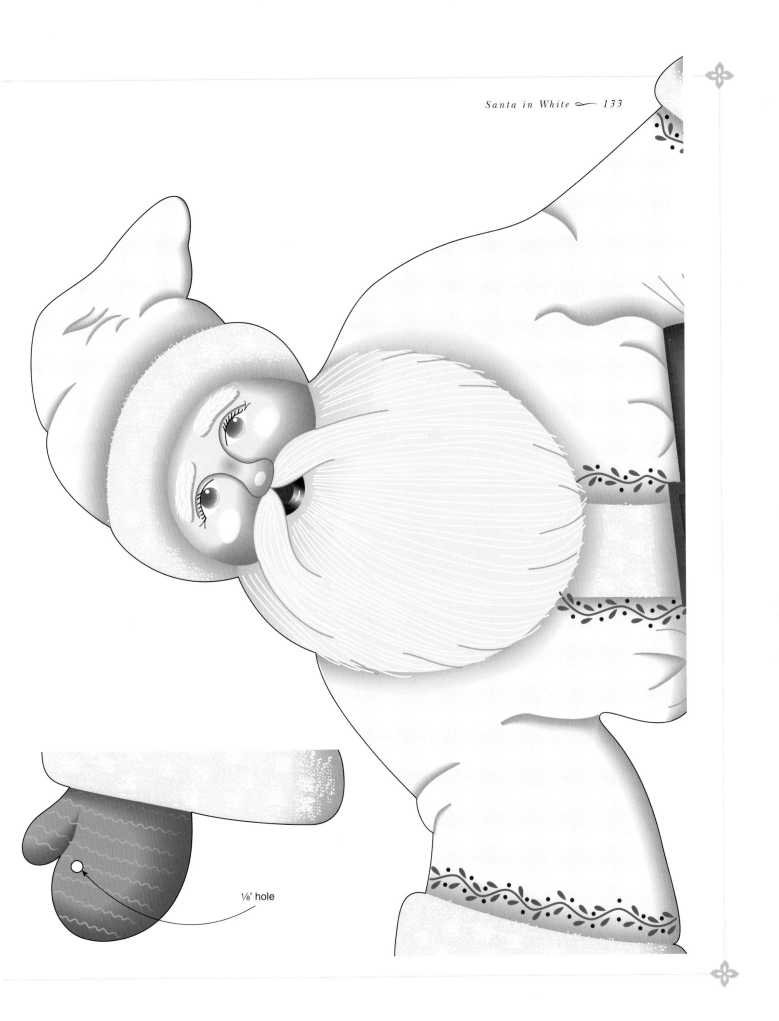

⅛' hole

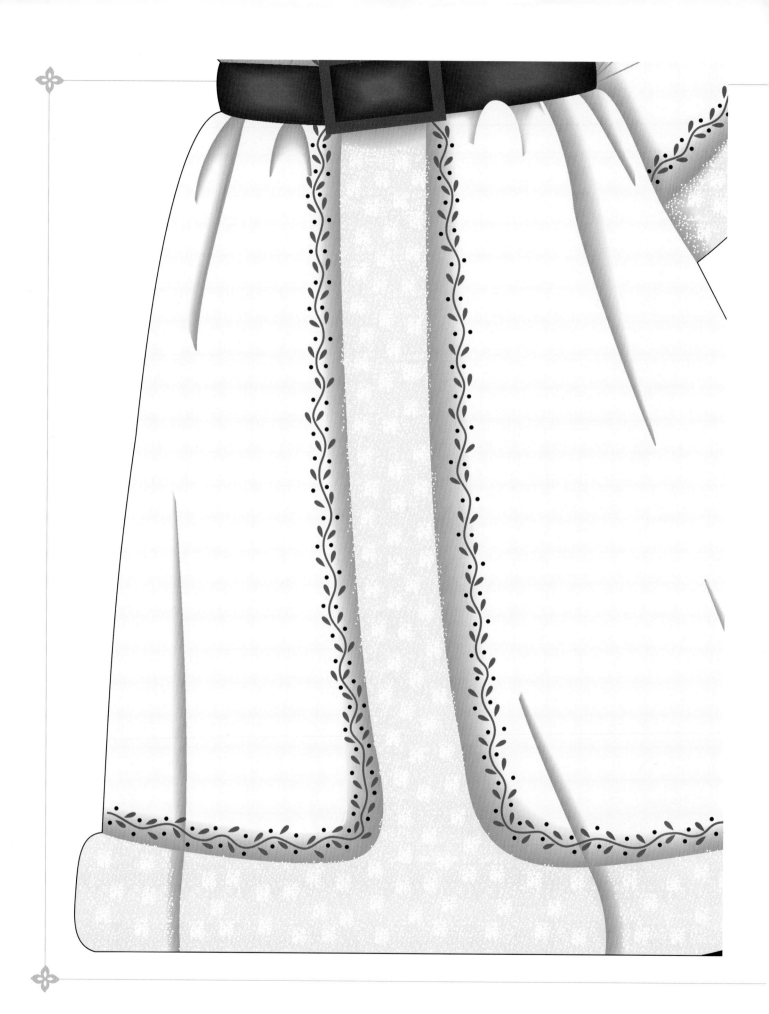

Quarter Base Pattern

Postcard
Santa Pillow

The finished pillow is 18½" square. ✦ *Designed by Nancy Kirk*
Photograph by Craig Anderson

MATERIALS

- 4 antique or reproduction postcards or other Santa pictures
- 2—8×11" sheets of photo transfer paper
- 2—9×12" pieces of bleached muslin
- 1⅛ yards of ecru brocade for the sashing and pillow back
- Assorted scraps of fancy fabrics (satin, brocade, and/or velvet)
- 4—7½" squares of sheer interfacing
- Assorted metallic threads
- Ecru sewing thread
- 18" pillow form

When old-fashioned needlework teams up with newfangled photo-transfer paper, the result is a crazy-quilt Santa pillow. Nancy Kirk used antique postcards and scraps of brocade. For a keepsake, substitute family pictures with Santa and remnants of holiday clothing.

PREPARE THE FABRICS

Following the manufacturer's instructions on the photo-transfer paper, make color photocopies of the postcard images and transfer them onto the muslin. Remember to set the copier to make a mirror image, or your postcards will appear reversed when transferred to fabric. Or have the postcards transferred at a copy shop.

Trim excess fabric from around the transferred images, leaving ¼" seam allowance. If desired, trim away portions of the postcard images to create irregular shapes. From the ecru brocade, cut two 19" square backs, two 2×7½" vertical sashing strips, one 2×16" horizontal sashing strip, two 2×16" side border strips, and two 2×19" strips for the top and bottom borders. Cut all of the remaining fancy fabrics into irregular shapes.

PIECE THE BLOCKS

For each block, pin the postcard transfer, right side up, in the center of one interfacing square (see Step 1, *right*). Choose a fancy-fabric shape and pin it, right sides together, to one edge of the transfer, aligning the straight edges. Sew through all layers. Turn the fancy fabric right side up and finger-press the seam (see Step 2). Select a second fancy-fabric shape and position it, right side down, across the seam of the first two fabrics, aligning the raw edges. Sew seam as before and finger-press open. Referring to Step 3, continue adding fancy fabric shapes, making sure each new shape covers the previous seam line until the interfacing square is covered. If necessary, turn the pieced block over and trim excess fancy fabrics even with the interfacing. The completed block should measure 7½" square. Repeat to make a total of four blocks. Press the blocks.

Referring to the diagram, *below*, use the metallic threads to work a line of featherstitches over each seam on the front of each pieced block. Vary the threads and stitches to compliment the adjoining fabrics.

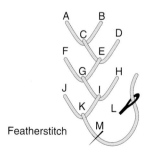

Featherstitch

ASSEMBLE THE PILLOW

Sew the long edge of each vertical sashing strip to the right-hand edge of a block. Sew the remaining long edge of each vertical sashing strip to the left edge of one remaining block to make rows. Press the seams toward the sashing strips. Sew a block row to each long edge of the horizontal sashing strip. Press the seams toward the sashing strip. Sew a vertical border strip to each side edge of the rows. Press the seams toward the border strips. Sew one remaining border strip to the top edge and one to the bottom to complete the pillow front. Press the seams toward the border strips.

Press one long edge of each back rectangle under ½". Topstitch close to the fold to form a hem. Fold the same edge under 3" and pin in place. With right sides facing, align the raw edges of one back piece with three raw edges of the pillow front. Repeat with the other back piece at the opposite edge of the pillow front so the hemmed edges are parallel and overlap about 9" in the center. Sew around the pillow. Trim the corners, turn the pillow cover right side out through the overlap, and press. Insert the pillow form. ✦

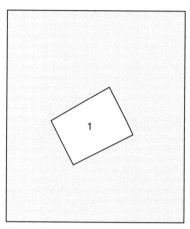

Step 1: Begin crazy-quilting with the fabric that has the postcard transfer on it.

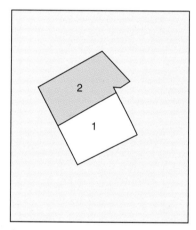

Step 2: Add fabric to one side, trimming as necessary.

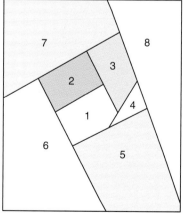

Step 3: Continue adding fabric as shown.

Santa Sitting on a
Snowball

Susan Brack and her daughter Rachel have made dozens of papier-mâché Santas like this impish fellow sitting on a snowball. If you prefer a larger—or smaller—Santa, Susan says it's easy to change his size. Read more about Susan on page 104.

MATERIALS

- Aluminum foil
- Dinner plate or cookie sheet
- 1-lb. package of gray or white Celluclay instant papier-mâché
- Toothpick or modeling tool
- Assorted paint brushes
- Acrylic paints: red, black, pale green, pale peach, white, cream, and blue
- Antiquing gel (optional)
- Acrylic varnish
- Crafts glue
- Glitter

PHOTO 1

The finished piece is 6" tall. ✦ *Designed by Susan and Rachel Brack*

Photographs by Craig Anderson

WORKING WITH INSTANT PAPIER-MÂCHÉ

It's best to mix a new batch of papier-mâché for each step of the process. Store any leftover mixture in the refrigerator, and add it to the next batch. Allow the figure to air-dry for several days before proceeding to the next step and for up to two weeks before painting. Drying time depends on the size of the project and the humidity.

SNOWBALL

Cover the plate or cookie sheet with aluminum foil. For the snowball, crumple another piece of foil into a ball approximately 3" in diameter. Mix about one-third of the papier-mâché mixture with water according to the manufacturer's directions. Use your hands to smooth the mixture about ¼" thick over the entire foil ball to form the snowball (see Photo 1, *above*). Let dry.

SANTA CLAUS

Mix a new batch of papier-mâché. Roll part of the mixture into two tubes, each about 2½" long, for the legs. Place the legs on the snowball, making sure they're firmly attached. Gently smooth the edges into the snowball to prevent them from separating as they dry.

Form two small wedges for the feet, and attach them to the ends of the legs. Smooth the edges into the legs and the snowball (see Photo 2, *opposite*).

Crumple another piece of foil into a narrow tube about 2" long. Cover the tube with papier-mâché to form the body and head. Shape the head into a point. Set the body onto the legs, and smooth the edges onto the snowball. Use a toothpick dipped in water to scribe details such as buttons, coat opening, and pockets. Let dry.

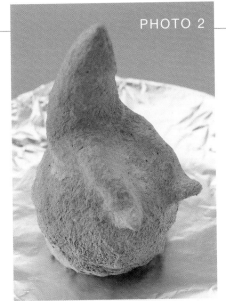

PHOTO 2

PHOTO 3

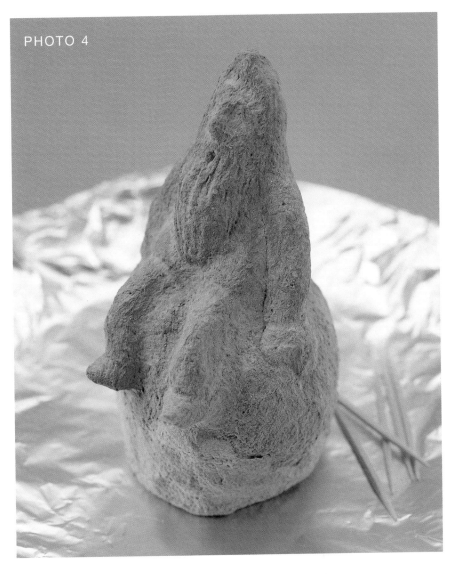

PHOTO 4

Mix a third batch of papier mâché. For the arms, roll two tubes long enough to reach from the shoulders to the snowball. Attach them to the body, smoothing as before (see Photo 3, *above*). Shape two mittens, and attach them to the ends of the arms.

For the face, make a flattened disc, and attach a small wedge of papier-mâché for the nose. Press it onto the head. Then shape a beard and attach it to the bottom of the face. Use a toothpick or other modeling tool to shape the features of the face and to add texture to the beard (see Photo 4, *above*). If desired, shape and add a bag of toys or fur strips to the coat. Allow the figure to dry thoroughly.

PAINTING

Using the photograph on *page 139* as a reference, paint the snowball and clothing first. Use pale peach to paint the face, adding a tiny amount of red to blush the cheeks. Paint white almond shapes for the eyes, and add a dot of blue in the center of each. Paint the beard, encircling the face, mustache, and eyebrows cream. Paint the mouth red. Sign and date the piece. Allow the paint to dry overnight.

If desired, apply antiquing gel and allow to dry. Brush a coat of acrylic varnish over the piece and let dry. To add glitter, brush a thin coat of crafts glue on the head, shoulders, toes, and on top of the snowball, and sprinkle glitter on the wet glue. Shake off excess glue and allow the glue to dry.✦

Redwork, the vivid embroidery in the colors of Santa's coat, must be his favorite form of stitchery. Simple materials—red floss and white muslin—mean these versatile Santa portraits stitch up quickly. Designer Cindy Taylor Oates framed them in quilt sashing to use as ornaments or package ties, but she says they also make great Christmas-card fronts.

Santa in
Redwork

Each ornament is 5⅛×5¾". ✦ Designed by Cindy Taylor Oates
Photographs by Craig Anderson

MATERIALS

- 2—9" squares of 100% cotton unbleached muslin
- ⅛" yard *each* of four 44"-wide red-and-cream cotton prints and plaids
- ¼ yard of 44"-wide red-and-cream cotton small plaid for backs and binding
- Red 03 Pigma marker
- Red cotton embroidery floss (DMC 304)
- Red crayon
- 2—6½×7½" pieces of cotton batting
- 2—6½×7½" pieces of stiff non-woven interfacing

STITCH THE DESIGN

Wash, dry, and press the muslin and cotton prints.

Use the Pigma marker to trace each design, *page 144,* onto a muslin square. *Do not* trace the dotted lines that indicate running stitches. Using two plies of floss, backstitch all the lines. For Santa's eyes, use two plies to make French knots. For the bear's eyes, use one ply to make French knots. Add running stitches as indicated on the patterns. Smudge a crayon lightly on the cheeks of each figure. When stitching is complete, press from the back.

SEW THE BLOCKS

Centering the design, trim the embroidered pieces to measure 4⅛×4¾". From each of the four red-and-cream prints and plaids, cut a 1½×44" strip, trimming away the

B A D C F E
Backstitch

1
2 French Knot

Running Stitch

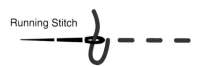

selvage at each end. From the red-and-cream plaid, cut two 6½×7½" rectangles and enough 1½"-wide bias strips to total 60".

For each ornament, layer an interfacing rectangle and a batting rectangle. Center an embroidered rectangle, right side up,

on the batting. Trim one of the red-and-cream 1½×44" strips to 4⅛" long. Align one long edge at the top of the embroidered rectangle, right sides together. Sew together, using a ¼" seam and stitching through all layers. Fold the strip to the right side and press.

From a second red-and-cream 1½×44" strip, cut a 5¾"-long strip. Sew the strip to one side of the embroidered rectangle and press. Continue around the block, adding a 5⅛"-long strip of a third print to the bottom edge and a 6¾"-long strip of the remaining print to the other side.

With wrong sides together, place the pieced block on the backing. Trim the block to measure 5⅛×5¾". Machine-stitch through all layers a scant ¼" from the raw edges.

FINISH THE EDGES

Sew the ends of the binding strips using diagonal seams to make one long piece; press the seams open. Fold the strip in half lengthwise and press. If desired, cut the 60" strip in half before binding the ornaments. Fold one end of the strip under ½". Beginning on one long side of an ornament, align the binding strip to the right side, mitering the corners. Braid two 3" strands (six plies) of floss together. Pin the ends to the top of the ornament. Turn the folded edge to the right side and slip-stitch to the back.✦

Grow your own long-necked gourds or pick some up at a farmer's market and create our easy-to-paint Gourd Santa. Designer Kathy Cornell is an avid gourd gardener who shares her tips for drying and cleaning them.

Gourd Santa

The finished Santa is 8½" tall. ✦ *Designed by Kathy Cornell*

Photograph by Craig Anderson

MATERIALS

- Long-necked ornamental gourd with 2×3" egg-shape bulb for the torso
- Long-necked ornamental gourd with 2"-diameter round bulb for the head
- 4 long-necked ornamental gourds with straight 3"–4" necks for the limbs
- Dremel Mototool with cutting wheel, router bit, sanding disk, and 1⁄16" drill bit
- Dust mask
- 150-grit sandpaper
- Damp cloth
- Crafts glue
- Pencil
- Acrylic paints: red iron oxide, pale peach, azure blue, metallic black, Inca gold, white, brown, and navy blue
- Assorted flat paintbrushes and small liner brush
- Spray varnish
- Long needle
- Red button thread
- 4—1⁄8"-diameter red doll buttons
- Jute cord (about 4 feet)
- Mandella wool for beard (available at craft stores)
- Thick white string or wool for the mustache and brows

DRYING THE GOURDS

After harvesting the ornamental gourds, place them in a single layer in a shallow cardboard box or on a cooling rack for 1 to 3 months (sometimes longer). Turn them every few days. When they're sufficiently dry, they'll be very light (about 10 percent of their original weight) and the seeds will rattle when the gourds are shaken.

CLEANING THE GOURDS

Immerse the gourds in warm soapy water (dish soap works well) for about 20 minutes, making sure that they're completely covered with water. If necessary, weight the gourds with a dinner plate to hold them down. After soaking, scrub well with steel wool or a plastic scrubber. Let them dry completely.

CUTTING THE GOURDS

With the dust mask on, use the Dremel tool with cutting wheel to cut the neck off the torso gourd, leaving a ½" stub for Santa's neck. Cut the neck off the head gourd, leaving a short stub for the peak of the cap. Use the router-bit attachment to make a hole in the opposite end of the head gourd and enlarge it with the sanding disk until it's large enough for Santa's neck to fit. Sand the head and torso gourds lightly with sandpaper. Wipe the dust off with a damp cloth. Let dry, then use crafts glue to secure the head to the torso.

For the limbs, use a pencil to mark the desired length for the arms and legs on the long-necked gourds. With the cutting wheel attachment, cut the necks from these gourds. Use the sanding disk to angle the cut edge of each limb so it fits against the torso gourd in the appropriate position. Sand lightly, wipe with a damp cloth, and let dry.

PAINTING THE SANTA

Apply two coats of red iron oxide to the arms and legs, the hat area and the torso, letting dry between coats. Paint the hands with azure blue, the boots and belt with metallic black, and the belt detail with Inca gold. Paint the face area with pale peach. Let dry.

Transfer the facial details. Mix a little red iron oxide with pale peach and lightly shade the cheeks. Use white to paint the almond eye shapes. Use brown paint and a liner brush to outline the eyes and nose; let dry. Paint the irises navy blue; let dry. Paint the center of each eye brown; let dry. Add a tiny dot of white to each upper-left eye center. Below the nose, paint a small mouth with red iron oxide; let dry. Spray all of the parts with two coats of varnish, letting it dry between coats.

Use ¹⁄₁₆" drill bit to make a hole at the top of each limb. Drill corresponding holes in the torso. Thread the long needle with red button thread. Holding the thread tail, begin on the inside of one arm, and thread the needle through the hole in the arm, both buttonholes of one button, the outside of the first arm, the body, the inside of the remaining arm, and both holes of the second button. Return the needle through the second arm and the body. Pull the arms close to the body and tie the thread tails together between the body and the arm. Attach the legs in the same manner.

Glue a small amount of Mandella wool around the face for a beard. For mustache and brows, glue on a small amount of white wool or string. Referring to the pattern, wrap and glue jute around the wrists, ankles, hat, and pom-pom.✦

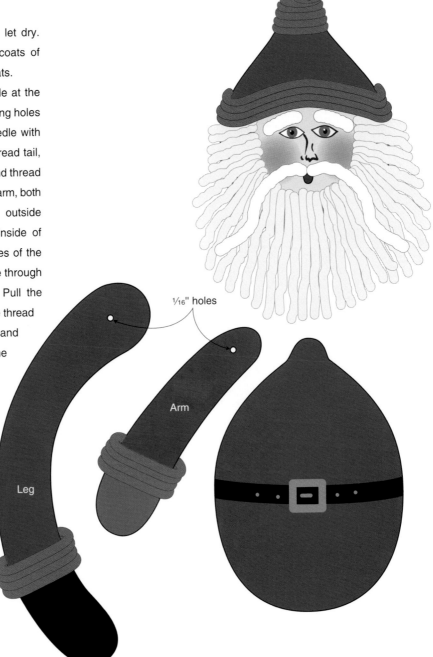

¹⁄₁₆" holes

Arm

Leg

Cranberry-Apple
Tea

Stained-Glass
Window Stars

Winter's Day
Espresso

Hot Spiced
Cider

For generations,
loving children, figuring wisely
that one last measure
of kindness on Christmas Eve
couldn't hurt their cause,
have left treats for Santa.

SWEET SENSATIONS

Sippers *for* Santa

ALTHOUGH COLD MILK AND SUGAR COOKIES
ARE STANDARD FARE IN MANY HOUSEHOLDS, SANTA MIGHT
APPRECIATE A CHANGE OF PACE.

Warm up the jolly old elf with one of the toasty trio of beverages pictured on *pages 148–149*. **Cranberry-Apple Tea** (recipe, *page 154*), a warm blend of spices, honey, tea, and apple juice, is perfect for chasing away the chills of sliding down chimneys. Besides, little helpers will get a kick out of watching the cranberries pop. Another sipper to give Santa pause is **Hot Spiced Cider** (recipe, *page 155*), quick to make on a busy and exciting night. **Winter's Day Espresso** (recipe, *page 153*) begins with a North Pole favorite, eggnog.

Or offer Santa a coffeehouse specialty, *opposite,* such as **Winter's Day Espresso, Spiced Orange Mocha,** laced with orange and spices, or soothing **Chocolate Cappuccino,** flavored lightly with crushed peppermint candies. Recipes are on *page 153–154.*

If you believe Santa needs a cool drink to refresh him along the way, especially in warm climates, he's sure to appreciate tropical-fruit-flavored **Minted Mango Tea,** ice-cream topped **Raspberry-Coffee Frappé,** and the fruity taste of **Citrus Raspberry Cooler**. Recipes are on *page 153*.

Look on *page 157* to discover a new cookie taste treat to accompany Santa's sippers. **Cherry-Coconut Drops,** appearing like colorful Christmas lights covered with fresh snow, are easy to fix. **Shortbread Sticks** provide a way for little helping hands to get a feel for the joys of holiday baking. There are no cookie cutters needed for this treat. In fact, a pizza cutter will make quick work of making the sticks. **Star Cookies** are super versatile. Decorate them in all-white, painted, or stained-glass-window styles. Recipes are on *pages 155–156.*

Oh, one more thing. It's a good idea to leave a bunch of carrots, too, for the reindeer. They work pretty hard as Santa's taxi service on this special night.

Written by Carol McGarvey ◆ *Food Styling by Diana Nolin* ◆ *Photographs by Scott Little*

Chocolate
Cappuccino

Winter's Day
Espresso

Spiced Orange
Mocha

Minted
Mango Tea

Raspberry-Coffee
Frappé

Citrus-
Raspberry
Cooler

REFRESHING COLD DRINKS

MINTED MANGO TEA

1 cup chopped refrigerated
  mango slices
1 cup pineapple juice
8 green tea bags
2 4-inch mint sprigs
4 cups boiling water
1 to 2 tablespoons sugar
Ice cubes

Place the chopped mango and pineapple juice in a blender container or food processor bowl. Cover and blend or process until smooth. Cover and refrigerated the pureed mixture.

Meanwhile, in a large glass bowl, pour boiling water over the tea bags and mint sprigs. Cover and let steep 5 minutes. Remove and discard the tea bags and mint sprigs. Cool, covered, for 1 hour. Chill for 2 hours.

Transfer the chilled tea to a 2-quart pitcher; add the pureed mango mixture and sugar. Stir until the sugar is dissolved.

To serve, pour the tea mixture into ice-filled glasses. Garnish each glass with an additional *mango slice* and a *pineapple star.* **Makes 6 (8-ounce) servings.**

CITRUS-RASPBERRY COOLER

5 raspberry tea bags
2 cups boiling water
½ cup sugar
2 cups cold water
⅓ cup frozen orange juice concentrate
  (½ of a 6-ounce container)
1 tablespoon lemon juice
1 2-liter bottle of club soda, chilled
Raspberry Ice (optional)

In a 3-quart heatproof glass pitcher, pour boiling water over the tea bags. Let steep 5 minutes. Remove and discard the tea bags. Stir in the sugar until dissolved. Stir in the cold water, frozen orange juice concentrate, and lemon juice. Chill until serving time.

To serve, pour the club soda down the sides of the pitcher. Break up the Raspberry Ice and add to the pitcher. **Makes 18 (8-ounce) servings.**

Raspberry Ice: Add water to a 9×13×2-inch baking pan to a depth of ¼ inch. Arrange fresh *raspberries* and strips of *lemon peel* in the water and freeze until firm. Add more water until the total depth is ½ inch and freeze until firm.

RASPBERRY-COFFEE FRAPPÉ

2 cups strong coffee, chilled
¼ cup raspberry-flavor syrup
½ cup half-and-half or light cream
18 ice cubes (about 2½ cups)
6 scoops of coffee-flavor ice cream
Chocolate shavings

Place *1 cup* of the coffee, the raspberry-flavor syrup, the half-and-half or light cream, and the ice cubes in a blender container. Cover and blend until the ice is finely crushed. Add the remaining coffee. Cover and blend on the lowest speed just until combined.

To serve, pour the coffee mixture into glasses. Top each glass with a scoop of coffee-flavor ice cream and chocolate shavings. **Makes 6 (6-ounce) servings.**

HOT DRINKS

WINTER'S DAY ESPRESSO
Shown on pages 148 and 151.

⅓ cup dairy eggnog
½ cup hot espresso or very
  strong coffee
1 to 2 teaspoons Irish-cream-flavor
  syrup for coffee
Whipped cream
Ground nutmeg

Place the eggnog in a large microwave-safe coffee mug. Microwave on 100 percent power (high) for 35 to 60 seconds or until hot. Add the hot espresso or coffee and syrup. Top with whipped cream and a sprinkling of nutmeg. **Makes 1 serving.**

SPICED ORANGE MOCHA

1 medium orange
2 inches stick cinnamon
7 whole cloves
2 cups water
2 cups milk
½ cup packed brown sugar
¼ cup unsweetened cocoa powder
2 tablespoons instant
   coffee crystals
¼ teaspoon rum extract
Orange curls (optional)

Remove peel from the orange using a vegetable peeler. Tie the orange peel, cinnamon, and cloves in a double-layer square of 100-percent-cotton cheesecloth.

Squeeze juice from the orange; add water, if necessary, to equal ⅓ cup. Combine the orange juice, spice bag, water, milk, brown sugar, and cocoa powder in a large saucepan. Bring to boiling; remove from heat. Stir in the coffee crystals. Cover; let stand 10 minutes. Remove the spice bag. Stir in rum extract. If desired, garnish each cup with an orange curl. **Makes 6 servings.**

CHOCOLATE CAPPUCCINO

½ cup whipping cream
3 tablespoons powdered sugar
½ cup finely chopped semisweet
   chocolate or finely chopped
   milk chocolate
½ cup crushed striped round
   peppermint candies
8 cups hot espresso or very
   strong coffee
Chocolate curls

Beat the whipping cream and powdered sugar with an electric mixer on low speed until soft peaks form; set aside.

Spoon *1 tablespoon each* chopped chocolate and peppermint candies into a coffee cup. Add hot espresso. Top with the whipped cream and chocolate curls. Serve at once. **Makes 8 servings.**

CRANBERRY-APPLE TEA

2 cups fresh cranberries
6 thin slices gingerroot
4 whole cloves
2 2-inch pieces stick cinnamon
4 cups water
¼ cup honey
4 tea bags
4 cups apple juice

Stir together cranberries, spices, and water in a large saucepan. Bring to boiling; reduce heat. Cook, uncovered, over medium heat for 3 to 5 minutes or just until cranberries begin to pop.

Remove from heat. Stir in honey; add tea bags. Strain cranberry mixture through a double thickness of 100-percent-cotton cheesecloth. Discard solids. Return strained mixture to the saucepan. Add apple juice; heat through. **Makes 8 cups.**

HOT SPICED CIDER

8 cups apple cider or apple juice
¼ to ½ cup packed brown sugar
6 inches stick cinnamon
1 teaspoon whole allspice
1 teaspoon whole cloves
Small apple slices

In a saucepan combine cider and brown sugar. For spice bag, tie cinnamon, allspice, and cloves in double layer of 100-percent-cotton cheesecloth. Add the spice bag to the cider mixture.

Bring to a boil; reduce heat. Cover and simmer for 10 minutes. Remove the spice bag; discard. Serve cider in mugs with small apple slices, if desired. **Makes 8 (about 8-ounce) servings.**

COOKIES

CHERRY-COCONUT DROPS

Shown on page 157.
1 7-ounce package (2⅔ cups) flaked coconut
2 tablespoons cornstarch
1 cup sweetened condensed milk
1 teaspoon vanilla
½ cup chopped red and/or green candied cherries

Grease and flour a cookie sheet; set aside. In a medium mixing bowl combine coconut and cornstarch. Stir in sweetened condensed milk and vanilla until mixture is combined. Stir in the chopped candied cherries.

Drop by small rounded teaspoonfuls about 1 inch apart on the prepared cookie sheet. Bake in a 325° oven for 12 to 15 minutes or until lightly browned on bottoms. Cool on cookie sheet for 1 minute. Transfer cookies to a wire rack; cool. **Makes about 24 cookies.**

SHORTBREAD STICKS

Shown on page 157.
1½ cups all-purpose flour
½ cup sifted powdered sugar
⅔ cup butter
2 tablespoons finely chopped candied ginger
¼ cup finely chopped sliced almonds
¼ cup candied red cherries, finely chopped
1 tablespoon granulated sugar

All-White Frosted Stars

In a medium mixing bowl, stir together flour and powdered sugar. Cut in butter until mixture resembles fine crumbs and starts to cling. Stir in candied ginger. Form the mixture into a ball; knead gently in bowl until smooth. On a lightly floured surface, roll the dough to a 14×6-inch rectangle (about ¼ inch thick).

In a bowl, stir together the almonds, cherries, and granulated sugar. Sprinkle evenly over dough; press in lightly. Using a knife or pizza cutter, cut into 28 6×½-inch strips. Place about ½ inch apart on an ungreased cookie sheet.

Bake in a 325° oven for 16 to 18 minutes or until bottoms of cookies just start to brown. Cool on cookie sheet 5 minutes. Transfer to wire racks; let cool. **Makes 28 sticks.**

STAR COOKIES

⅓ **cup butter**
⅓ **cup shortening**
¾ **cup sugar**
1 **teaspoon baking powder**
1 **egg**
1 **tablespoon milk**
1 **teaspoon vanilla**
2 **cups all-purpose flour**
Powdered-Sugar Frosting (optional)

Beat butter and shortening with an electric mixer on medium to high speed for 30 seconds. Add sugar, baking powder, and dash *salt;* beat

until combined. Beat in egg, milk, and vanilla. Beat in as much of the four as you can with the mixer. Stir in any remaining flour with a wooden spoon. Divide dough in half. Cover and chill for 3 hours.

Powdered-Sugar Frosting: Combine 1 cup sifted *powdered sugar* and 1 tablespoon *milk.* Stir in additional milk, 1 teaspoon at a time, until of drizzling consistency.

All-White Frosted Stars

Roll one portion of dough at a time to ¼-inch thickness on a lightly floured surface. Cut into stars using 2½- or 3-inch cutters. Using a wide spatula, transfer cutouts to an ungreased cookie sheet. Bake in a 375° oven for 7 to 8 minutes or until edges are firm and bottoms are very lightly browned. Cool on wire racks.

Using a narrow spatula, frost cookies almost to the edge with Powdered-Sugar Frosting; let stand until frosting is set. Pipe additional frosting around edges of stars or where you plan to add *white decorating candies.* While frosting is wet, sprinkle with candies. Store in a tightly covered container with waxed paper between layers of cookies. **Makes about 30.**

Painted Stars

Roll, cut out, and bake as directed *at left.* Make two recipes of Powdered-Sugar Frosting. Tint one recipe with *liquid food coloring.* Frost cooled cookies, one or two at a time, with untinted frosting. While frosting is wet, add dots of colored frosting and pull a clean toothpick through the dots to make a design. Let stand till frosting is set. Store in a tightly covered container with waxed paper between layers of cookies. **Makes about 30.**

Stained-Glass-Window Stars

Roll one portion of dough at a time to ¼-inch thickness on a lightly floured surface. Cut into stars using 2½- or 3-inch cutters. Using a wide spatula, transfer cutouts to a foil-lined cookie sheet. Using a 1-inch star cutter or desired hors d'oeuvre cutters, cut out shapes in centers of stars. Finely crush 3 ounces *hard candy* (about ½ cup). Spoon some candy into the center of each star to fill holes. Bake in a 375° oven for 7 to 8 minutes or until edges are firm. Move foil and cookies to wire rack; cool on foil. When cookies are completely cool, peel away foil. Store tightly covered. **Makes about 30.**

Shortbread
Sticks

Painted
Stars

Painted
Stars

Stained-
Glass
Window
Stars

All-White
Frosted Stars

Cherry-Coconut
Drops

Sources

Timeless Memorabilia

Santa in Song, *pages 36–41*
The Golden Glow of Christmas Past, 6401 Winsdale
St., Golden Valley, MN 55427; www.goldenglow.org.

Devoted Collectors

A Lifetime of Collecting Christmas, *pages 44–49*
Scott's Antiques, 414/332-8184.

Master Crafters

Adrift with Marge Mable, *pages 58–63*
Folk Art Shop, 333 5th St., West Des Moines, IA 50265,
515/274-1419.

The Careful Carver, *pages 64-69*
Sylvester Dietrich's work is available at New Haven
Antique Mall, 117–119 Front St., New Haven, MO
63068, 573/237-2420 and Timeless Traditions, 104
Elm St., Washington, MO 63090, 636/390-8840.

Face Value, pages 76–83
www.audreyswarz.com.

In the Details, *pages 84-89*
Elizabeth Raol, 119 W. 16th Ave., Spokane, WA 99203;
e-mail: Oldworld fathers@aol.com.

Wonders of Walnut Ridge, *pages 90-95*
For the names of retailers in your area who offer
Walnut Ridge Collectibles, call 800/275-1765.

Santa's Student, *pages 96-103*
Pipka's Gallery and Gifts, 920/854-4392;
www.pipka.com.

An Elf in Disguise, *pages 104-111*
Susan Brack, 6388 South Bath Springs Road, Liberty,
IN 47353. For Gallerie II retailers in your area, call
888/909-5656.

Everything New Is Old Again, *pages 112-117*
Toys in the Attic, 888/253-0020; e-mail:
toysintheattic@sympatico.ca.

Personal Expressions

Santa's Gifts, *pages 120-125*
Wool felt—National Nonwovens, P.O. Box 150,
Easthampton, MA 01027, 800/333-3469.

Santa in Checks, *pages 126-129*
DecoArt, 800/367-3047; www.decorart.com.

Santa in White, *pages 130-135*
Delta Technical Coatings, 800/423-4135;
www.deltacrafts.com.

Santa Sitting on a Snowball, *pages 139-141*
Celluclay—Activa Products, Inc., 800/255-1910;
www.activa-products.com.

Gourd Santa, *pages 145-147*
Dremel Tools, 800-437-3635; www.dremel.com.

COLLECTION

Editor-in-Chief	Beverly Rivers

Creative Director	Daniel Masini
Senior Editor	Eve Mahr
Associate Art Director	Carrie Topp
Associate Art Director/Photography	Patty Crawford
Editorial Coordinator	Carol Linnan
Administrative Assistant	Mary Johnson
Contributing Copy Editors	Dave Kirchner, Margaret Smith

Publishing Director	William R. Reed
Publisher	Maureen Ruth
Group Consumer Marketing Director	Liz Bredeson
Marketing Manager	Becky Nash
Business Manager	Kristen Eaton
Production Manager	Douglas M. Johnston
Book Production Managers	Pam Kvitne, Marjorie J. Schenkelberg

Vice President	Jerry Ward

Chairman and CEO	William T. Kerr

Chairman of the Executive Committee	E.T. Meredith III

Meredith Publishing Group

Publishing Group President	Stephen M. Lacy
President, Magazine Group	Jerry Kaplan
Corporate Solutions	Michael Brownstein
Creative Services	Ellen de Lathouder
Manufacturing	Bruce Heston
Consumer Marketing	Karla Jeffries
Operations	Dean Pieters
Finance	Max Runciman

For editorial questions, please write:
Better Homes and Gardens® Santa Claus Collection, Vol. 3
1716 Locust St., GA 307, Des Moines, IA 50309-3023

Printing Number and Year: 5 4 3 2 1   05 04 03 02 01
ISSN: 1524-9794   ISBN: 0-696-21367-2

Believe!